S0-ARL-554

A GALLERY OF
GHOSTS

A GALLERY OF GHOSTS

Andrew MacKenzie

AN ANTHOLOGY OF REPORTED EXPERIENCE

Introductory dialogue with Rosalind Heywood,
Vice-President of the Society for Psychical Research

CHICAGO HEIGHTS FREE PUBLIC LIBRARY

TAPLINGER PUBLISHING COMPANY | NEW YORK

133.1
M 15
c . 1

First published in the United States in 1973 by
TAPLINGER PUBLISHING CO., INC.
New York, New York

Copyright © 1972 by Andrew MacKenzie
All rights reserved. Printed in the U.S.A.

No part of this book may be reproduced or transmitted in any form or by any means, electronic or mechanical, including photocopy, recording, or any information storage and retrieval system now known or to be invented, without permission in writing from the publisher, except by a reviewer who wishes to quote brief passages in connection with a review written for inclusion in a magazine, newspaper, or broadcast.

Library of Congress Catalog Card Number: 73-2019

ISBN 0-8008-3122-5

ACKNOWLEDGEMENTS

Copyrighted material from which permission to quote has been granted:

Quotations from the *Journal* and *Proceedings* of the Council of the Society for Psychical Research, London, are made with the Council's permission.

My First Hundred Years by Margaret Murray. Reprinted with the permission of William Kimber and Co. Ltd.

Pen to Paper by Pamela Frankau. Copyright © 1961 by Pamela Frankau. Reprinted with the permission of Monica McCall, IFA.

Bugles and a Tiger: A Volume of Autobiography by John Masters. Copyright © 1956 by Bengal-Rockland Inc. Reprinted by permission of the Viking Press, Inc.

Black Beech and Honeydew by Ngaio Marsh. Copyright © 1965 by Ngaio Marsh Ltd. Reprinted with the permission of Harold Ober Associates, Ltd.

A Hind in Richmond Park by W. H. Hudson. Reprinted with the permission of The Royal Society for the Protection of Birds and the Society of Authors.

Trials in Burma by Maurice Collis. Reprinted with the permission of A. D. Peters and Co.

Portrait of my Victorian Youth by Alice Pollock. Reprinted with the permission of Johnson Publications Ltd.

The Candle of Vision by George Russell (A.E.). Reprinted with the permission of Mr. Diarmuid Russell and A. M. Heath and Company.

Memories, Dreams, Reflections by C. G. Jung. Edited by Aniela Jaffe. Translated by Richard and Clara Winston. Copyright © 1962, 1963 by Random House, Inc. Reprinted with the permission of Pantheon Books, a Division of Random House, Inc.

Can We Explain the Poltergeist? by A. R. G. Owen. Reprinted with the permission of the author and Garrett Publications/Helix Press.

Early Reminiscences by Sabine Baring-Gould. Reprinted with the permission of Hutchinson Publishing Group Ltd.

Left Hand, Right Hand! by Sir Osbert Sitwell. Copyright 1943, 1944 by Sir Osbert Sitwell. Reprinted with the permission of Atlantic-Little, Brown.

Green Memory by L. A. G. Strong. Reprinted with the permission of A. D. Peters and Co.

Journey from Obscurity, Wilfred Owen 1893–1918 by Harold Owen. The quotation from Vol. 3, *War*, is reprinted with the permission of Oxford University Press.

Det Ockulta Problemet by John Björkhem. Reprinted with the permission of J. A. Lindblads Förlag.

Apparitions by G. N. M. Tyrell. Reprinted with the permission of Gerald Duckworth and Co. Ltd.

Contents

	Foreword	7
1	Dialogue with Rosalind Heywood	13
2	What I Believe about Ghosts *Margaret Murray*	20
3	A Ghost Seen in a Mirror *Pamela Frankau*	26
4	The Ghosts of India *John Masters*	32
5	The Boy with the Flowers *Ngaio Marsh*	37
6	Faces in the Wind *W. H. Hudson*	40
7	The Guardian of the Treasure *Maurice Collis*	45
8	Pictures in the Crystal *Alice Pollock*	48
9	Vision in a Ruined Chapel *George Russell (A.E.)*	56
10	The Walkers by the Tower *C. G. Jung*	62
11	The Dream House *Augustus Hare*	69
12	The Bottle-Breaking Case *Cesare Lombroso*	72
13	The Sauchie Poltergeist *A. R. G. Owen*	78
14	The Worksop Case *Frank Podmore*	90
15	The Haunting of Lew House *Sabine Baring-Gould*	111
16	A Family Ghost *Osbert Sitwell*	123
17	The Return *L. A. G. Strong*	128
18	The Apparition in my Cabin *Harold Owen*	139
19	The Ghost of Grandfather Bull *The Earl of Balfour and J. G. Piddington*	144
20	Did Harry Price Return? *John Björkhem*	150

Foreword

The twenty principal cases in this anthology of ghostly or visionary experiences are taken in the main from biographies and autobiographies. Only five, 'The Bottle-Breaking Case', 'The Sauchie Poltergeist', 'The Worksop Case', 'The Ghost of Grandfather Bull' and 'Did Harry Price Return?' are from books or other publications concerned with psychical research. It was clear to me after I had read the assembled cases that many of them were similar to others I had recorded in my earlier books or psychical research or had come across in the serious studies published by the Society for Psychical research (SPR).

Unlike the ghost stories of fiction, which have a beginning, a middle and an end and deal with dramatic happenings involving revenge or remorse or, for some reason which has never been clear to me, with the observance of anniversaries, the true ghost story is fragmentary and often apparently meaningless. But there is a pattern that may be discerned in such cases when one has studied enough of them. In order to show that many of the cases in this anthology are not just isolated incidents, to be regarded with suspicion or misapprehension, I have included for purposes of comparison similar ones from the literature of the SPR and my own collection of cases, a number of which have not been published before.

I should explain that I am responsible for the heading of the chapters, not the authors from whose books these cases are taken.

This book may be read on two levels: as an anthology and, I trust, as a study in psychichal research. Although I comment in detail on some of the cases, they have not been put 'under the microscope' as they would be if the purpose of the book were an assessment of evidential material. For instance, John Masters quotes a story told to him by an unnamed friend, 'an officer of Indian cavalry'. The psychical researcher would normally ask, 'Who is this friend?' and then obtain from him a first-hand account. If I pursued this course quite a different book would have resulted. I do not think I need to labour this point.

I was struck by the nature of the little group of what I call 'return' cases which comprise the last five chapters, beginning with Osbert Sitwell's 'A family ghost ' I suggest that these may be read in conjunction with some of the experiences given by Rosalind Heywood in my introductory dialogue with her and also with the findings, published in the 2 October 1971 issue of the *British Medical Journal*, of Dr W. Dewi Rees, a Welsh general practitioner, who talked to 293 of his patients who had lost their marriage partners through death. Dr Rees said that widows and widowers who sense the presence of their former marriage partner are in no way unusual. Nearly half the patients had had some sensation of the presence of their spouse and in many it had persisted over several years, although over all the tendency was for the sensation to become less frequent. More than ten per cent of those questioned had spoken to or heard the voice of his or her partner, and a similar proportion had seen the apparition of their partner. Very few of the patients had spoken to their families about the matter, often because of fear of ridicule or because the experience was felt to be a private matter.

Confirmation of Dr Rees's finding is given in a Pelican original, *Dying* (1967), by Dr John Hinton, Professor of Psychiatry at the Middlesex Hospital School. He says:

It is a dramatic but quite common event for the bereaved to have the experience of apparently seeing or hearing the dead person.

Quite normal people, grieving over their loss, have glimpses of the person who has died. They may hear the familiar voice, perhaps saying their name, or recognize the footsteps or customary noises about the house. Ususally it is soon realized that this is a trick of the senses, but the experience is often extraordinarily vivid and apparently real. People having such hallucinations may wonder if they are going mad, but it usually comforts them to know that many other sane people have similar experiences following bereavement.

Professor Hinton maintains that ' the unconscious hope or the extreme desire for the loved person still to be alive may be conducive to hallucinations of his presence – in other words, cause and effect'. However, what can one make of a case like that reported by Harold Owen or Lord Brougham, to mention only two of the many on record, when a person sees the apparition of a friend or relative or someone with whom there is an emotional bond, not knowing that this person has recently died? Some mechanism other than cause and effect, based on conscious awareness of an event, is in operation here. It is possible, as Rosalind Heywood tentatively suggests, that the deceased *may* have some part in what is taking place. The relevance of such cases to what has been called the survival hypothesis is obvious, but I believe that we do not yet have enough evidence to come to a firm conclusion on whether we survive bodily death and if so in what form and for how long. I am not taking into consideration here factors of religious faith. This book has been written largely in collaboration with Rosalind Heywood, whose works on psychical research[1] are so well known. For some years she had been collecting cases for an anthology, but her health did not permit her to continue with the project. She was kind enough to let me use some of her cases and I have added a slightly larger number of cases collected by me from other sources. The comments on the cases are mine, so any reader

[1] *The Sixth Sense* (1959) and *The Infinite Hive* (1964), both published by Chatto and Windus and in Pan paperbacks.

who disagrees with them should not blame Mrs Heywood.

I am grateful to Mr George Zorab of The Hague for his advice on poltergeist cases – there are three in this book – and, as always, to Mr G. W. Lambert for his advice at various times.

A GALLERY OF
GHOSTS

I

Dialogue with
Rosalind Heywood

A.M. A great many people believe that a study of apparitions and ghosts shows an undue preoccupation with the stuff of folklore, superstition and legend and that it serves no purpose beyond that of entertainment. This view cannot be taken by anyone who has studied seriously the literature of the SPR and in particular G. N. M. Tyrrell's masterly work, *Apparitions*, or *Six Theories about Apparitions*, a co-operative report by Professor Hornell Hart and associated collaborators in the international project for research on ESP projection.[1] I share Tyrrell's view that psychical research helps us to form new qualitative ideas about the elements and processes of personality. However, let us get on to a less formal form of discussion. I have never seen a ghost, possibly because I am a poor visualizer, but you have. Would you care to tell me about your experiences?

R.H. Well, they were of two different types. The first visual experience I had was the apparition of a living person. He was a man with whom I was much in love, and he was in love with me. We were in different countries. I was living in a tent in Macedonia. When I woke up one morning he was standing in the entrance of the tent, perfectly clear and perfectly normal. And after a minute or two he vanished. I also had a letter from him about the same time saying that I had come into his room in Paris and sat down near him and talked to him. And he simply added, ' It *was* you.'

[1] *Proceedings* of the SPR (May 1956).

Well now, it sounds rather silly to say, but that is what I call a live ghost, one with apparent intention. What I call the ordinary apparition seems aimless. I have only once had a visual experience of one of these, though I have often ' felt ' them; and it was, oddly enough, in a big modern house in Johannesburg. We had just returned from the cinema, and I came out of the billiards room by myself into a passage. The family were all at the other end of the house and I knew all the servants had gone home and the house was locked up. Suddenly, to my surprise, a shadow fell between me and the passage light. I looked up quickly to see who it was and there was a man dressed in long, what you would call more or less oriental, clothes. I was immensely surprised because I knew there was no such man there. A moment afterwards he was gone. I wasn't in the least frightened, but afterwards I did notice that I felt cold about my solar plexus area. Later on I told my relations with whom I was staying about this, and apparently other people also, independently, had seen this figure. It took no notice of me and I had no feeling of ' intention ' on its part.

A.M. That is most interesting. Have you ever felt that someone is with you – what may be called a ' presence ' – but have not had a visual impression of the person concerned?

R.H. Oh, yes, that is the way I nearly always have such experiences, and I noticed an interesting thing when I was thinking them over the other day. The apparent presences *with intention* have, all but two, been people who, like myself, were interested in psychical research. The other two had very good reasons for turning up as they both wanted help given to their own relations.

A.M. In what way would you say that ghosts are ' real '? Do you think this is a fair question?

R.H. Well, I am not at all sure that it is a question that makes sense, because before asking it you would have to say what you mean by 'real'. I mean, if you were a materialist philosopher you might say that nothing was real but a focus of energy which you could call an ultimate particle or what have you. But if you mean real in the sense of inducing a conscious experience I would say that ghosts are certainly real, simply because many people I know, and I myself, and others I have read about and whom I believe to be truthful, have experienced them. But what causes such experiences is quite a different question: in what further sense, I mean, are they real? As I said, I couldn't answer that question until we had very carefully defined what we mean by 'real'.

A.M. This leads me on to the question of consciousness. In what way would you say that apparitions are vehicles of consciousness?

R.H. Well, again, as far as I am concerned that is a much more complicated question than it seems to be, because as I have already said I am not at all sure that there is only one kind of apparition. Incidentally, instead of the words apparition or ghost I would like to say visible or invisible presences. Now, of the presences that I *feel* I have experienced (whether I was right or wrong I don't know), some have shown intention, and I would be inclined to look on them as vehicles of consciousness. But others, what I call aimless ghosts, seem to wander about a particular area conscious of nothing – certainly not of the living people in the room. I think that they may well be quite a different type of phenomenon from the presences which seem to show intention. It may be that the strong emotions of some past inhabitant of a place have left some unknown type of impression on it, to which certain people are sensitive. I have known of 'ghosts' of living persons being seen in places where they used to live. Perhaps they were thinking of those places at the time. Also, one may telepathically pick up the tradition, believed by people living near by, that there is a ghost in a certain place.

A.M. I am most interested in the question of purpose and so, I believe, are a great many other people. What is your opinion of this? Are these appearances in many instances purposeful?

R.H. Well, again, that is terribly complicated. I think I will concentrate for the moment on cases where it has appeared to me that the presence had a definite purpose – or, as I said, intention. For instance, not long ago a great friend of mine died unexpectedly and I got a bad shock when I saw his obituary notice in *The Times*. A few days afterwards he appeared to turn up – invisibly – and conveyed to me urgently, 'I want you to telephone my wife.' Now I only knew her very slightly, as she lived at the other end of England; I had written her a note of sympathy and she had answered, and it seemed to be an extraordinary and pushing thing for me to ring her up just for no reason at all, merely to talk. I felt very much embarrassed, and also very extravagant. However, the apparent presence was so insistent that I did telephone, right across England, and we talked freely for a long time. I wrote to her again and telephoned again and again. Three weeks later she wrote to me: 'I would like you to know that if you hadn't rung me up and talked as you did, and written, I think I would have gone off my rocker. Out of tact nobody would speak to me of John, and the one thing I wanted to do was to talk about him.'

Another quite short incident has happened within the last year. A friend of mine died and I got the impression as from him that he wanted me to write to a friend of his, a very distinguished man, and let him know that all was satisfactory as regards his work. Again I was extremely embarrassed, as I didn't know this man very well and felt he would think 'silly woman' because, no more than I, was he convinced of survival. However, I did write, with many apologies, and he replied that he was delighted to get the message; as it happened, at the time when I sent it he had been very busy dealing with his dead friend's writings. Well, here again you see, I can't tell. I am quite neutral about survival. I don't know if people survive or if they don't, but I give the apparent presences of my friends the benefit of the doubt. At the same time in this case it may have been the fact that this distinguished man was working on my friend's papers that caused me to receive a telepathic 'signal' from him which I interpreted as coming from my dead friend – I can't tell. But I think it is exceedingly important that people who do get impressions of the presence of their dead friends should treat them as people, rather than ignore them and say, 'This is all nonsense.' After all, if you are mistaken, if there is no such thing as survival, you have merely made a fool of yourself, and what does that matter? But if they *are* there, and they *do* want to make contact, it's appalling to think that one might cut them – ignore them. Don't you think so?

A.M. I agree. What you are suggesting then is that we should treat these experiences as natural ones and not something of which we should be afraid.

R.H. I feel very strongly, not only that we should treat them as natural, but that they *are* natural. That doesn't mean that I know *what* they are; but at the same time I am convinced that they are natural. And, what is more, I find that the vast majority of people who have them moderately frequently feel them to be as normal as any other experience. Not only that, but small children who may have them seem to take them for granted. The other day a friend of mine told me that after her father had died her little girl of seven remarked, 'Oh, there is an old gentleman sitting on the stool, Mummy', and then she described her late grandfather. Well, that was that, there was an old gentleman sitting on the stool. What was odd about that?

A.M. It is interesting that you should have reported the experience of a child. I wonder if many other children have such experiences but they don't come to light. Could there be a reason for this?

R.H. I think there is a very good reason, which is that if children mention 'a ghost' most grown-ups say, 'Don't be naughty and make things up', and may even show signs of fear. The well-known sensitive, Phoebe Payne, told me that when she was a young child and her much-loved grandmother died, just as the funeral procession was about to set forth she said to her parents, 'But Mummy, Daddy, Grannie isn't in that box, Grannie is here playing with me.' Apparently this wasn't at all well received.

A.M. I have come across some interesting theories lately about apparitions. In her book *Out-Of-The-Body Experiences*[2] Celia Green draws attention a number of times to the parallelism between out-of-the-body experiences and apparitional experiences. For instance, the 'realism' of an out-of-the-body experience breaks down when the subject attempts to touch or handle something like an electric light switch. He finds that his hand goes right through it. The same thing happens when the percipient of an apparition tries to touch it. Perhaps more to the point is the suggestion which Renée Haynes makes in the review *Twentieth Century* that the psyche works in accordance with a self-portrait, and if the body image is in fact a man's habitual picture of himself, it is possibly this picture that is transmitted in telepathic hallucinations, and even in hauntings. May I put it this way: we all have our own idea of what we look like, and this image can get 'fixed', as it were, to a house and be picked up by somebody suitably sensitive at a later date. What do you think of this?

R.H. That is more or less one of the possibilities I mentioned earlier. I think that it is one of many and quite plausible. But, frankly, the more I have these experiences, the more I feel that

[2]Institute of Psychophysical Research (Oxford 1968)

we are not asking the right questions about them. I don't know what these questions should be, but I'm convinced that until we ask them we shall not get the right answers. I entirely agree that the image-making faculty of the psyche may be able to create permanent images. In fact, Professor H. H. Price suggests something of the kind in one of his important studies of ESP [extra-sensory perception], but I am tentative about imprisoning myself in any particular view because it seems to me that we don't yet know enough to do that. There are so many views, all of which have a certain degree of plausibility.

I want such *experiences*, whether visual, auditory or the awareness of invisible presences, to be treated quite simply as widespread natural psychological phenomena, to which so-called 'normal' people as well as 'sensitives' are prone. I want a percipient to be able to report what he or she has experienced as easily as if it had been a fox in a suburban garden, without being labelled 'mad' for doing so. I was recently told by the headmistress of a small infants' private school that more than one of her little pupils spoke of seeing people who were invisible to grown-ups and she mentioned this to the school doctor and a psychiatrist friend of hers. They both made it plain to her that she herself seemed to be mentally unbalanced.

I am sure that the way ahead is, as the great psychologist Sir Cyril Burt suggested, to treat all so-called paranormal phenomena as normal psychological phenomena and to study, assess and compare them as such. He puts this view at length in his two outstanding studies of the subject[3] and I hope that these will be more and more read and studied in the future.

[3] (a) 'Psychology and Parapsychology' in *Science and ESP,* J. R. Smythies (Routledge 1967) and (b) 'Psychology and Psychical Research' (the Myers Memorial Lecture) *Proc.* of SPR (1968).

2

What I Believe about Ghosts

MARGARET MURRAY

In the matter of ghosts, I believe quite seriously in apparitions though I do not accept the idea that they are living beings. There is comparatively little credible evidence, not actually enough to make the real meaning of the apparition clear. As a working hypothesis I suggest that they are a form of photograph, literally 'light writing'. Modern science has revealed some unexpected constituents of the atmosphere. Oxygen can be isolated and used in hospitals, by mountaineers and flight-pilots. Neon can be isolated and used commercially in cheap illumination. Then there are the invisibles, such as the rays which apparently pour upon the earth, X-rays, now common in medical work, cosmic rays, and probably many others which are being gradually discovered. Now that our atmosphere and space are being subjected to closer investigation, many of our now inexplicable phenomena may be explained in the future.

As this phenomenon of a so-called ghost is known to occur in many parts of the world, it is worth noting that it is more common in moist climates rather than in the drier ones. Thus, Scotland and Ireland have a considerably larger number of apparitions than England. In some parts of India where the atmosphere is, at least for some months of the year, steamily moist, ghosts abound, both indigenous and foreign. In the dry climate of Egypt and in the desert lands there is, as far as I know, no record, ancient or modern, of such apparitions. There may be *jinn* and *afreets*, but no ghosts. This seems to show that the conditions of the atmosphere should always be noted by a ghost-seer. Also whether there is an unusual amount of electricity, as before a thunderstorm.

It is noticeable that ghosts seldom, if ever, occur except in rooms or sheltered places. It is a remarkable point that the figure is always clothed in the garments that he or she was generally seen in; this is to me strongly suggestive of a photograph, a writing caused by light on some combination of the constituents of the air. A machine for catching the light-waves on a specially prepared surface is well-known as a photographic camera.

It should be remembered that, though the light-waves are recorded on a prepared surface, the result is not visible till the surface is specially treated; otherwise the surface (glass or film) remains blank. I suggest that this is also the case with apparitions. It is possible that the natural process of developing the negative may take a long time. Another point to note is the very restricted area in which the ghost is seen. If in a room it never goes outside that room; if out of doors, it never comes indoors; and you would never meet a ghost a quarter of a mile from its natural haunt. The suddenness of its disappearance suggests a current of air blowing away the particles on which it is imprinted. In its similarity to a photograph is the fact that it appears to fade in course of time, appearing less frequently. Towards the end of its 'existence', it will only appear in exceptional atmospheric conditions, such as just before an electrical storm.

The greater number of ghosts of the present day belong to the twentieth century. There are some of the nineteenth century, but those of the eighteenth century now occur only in houses in unusually lonely places, where there is little traffic and therefore little displacement of the air. There is at present no evidence from reliable witnesses as to whether a ghost appears at regular intervals or . . . only in certain conditions of the atmosphere. There is some evidence from two witnesses having seen an apparition when together but this, like all reliable evidence, is rare. And there is, as far as I know, no reliable photograph of a ghost.

As an illustration of a 'typical' ghost here is an account from a reliable eyewitness trained in exact observation. Mrs Marion Dansie, M.B., B.S., was a patient in the Woolavington Wing of the Middlesex Hospital, in a single room, in early May 1936. There were two windows; the door was in the opposite wall and opened into the room towards the foot of the bed, so that the patient lying in bed was screened from the corridor outside. The staff nurse on duty was an especially conscientious girl, very popular with all the patients.

One morning Mrs Dansie was lying awake about 5 a.m. It was a dull cloudy morning but the electric light was not on. Both windows were wide open, the door was closed but not shut. Mrs Dansie saw the door apparently pushed open from outside and the nurse walked in smiling and nodding to Mrs Dansie. The figure came round the door and stood at the side of the bed near the foot. Mrs Dansie said, 'Good morning. How nice to see you, but why are you on duty now?' As she spoke the figure vanished. When the day nurses came on duty this staff nurse was not among them, and Mrs Dansie was told that she had been taken ill in the night and had been taken to the sick nurses' ward. The end of this story is quite wrong if judged by the Christmas-tale type of ghost story, for both Mrs Dansie and the nurse recovered completely.

This account is taken from *My First Hundred Years* (William Kimber 1963) by Dr Margaret Murray, the distinguished archaeologist, Egyptologist and authority on witchcraft. She died on 14 November 1963 in her 101st year.

Let us consider first of all the experience of Mrs Dansie and the strange appearance of the staff nurse at an unusually early hour. This is a fairly typical example of an apparition of the living. It is possible that the nurse, a conscientious girl, was lying awake in the sick nurses' ward thinking of her patients, visiting, as it were, the ward in her mind; and that in a way that is not understood this was ' picked up ' by Mrs Dansie in the form of the apparition of the girl.

Dr Murray was a distinguished scholar and her views deserve respect, but possibly those on ghosts were derived more from folklore (she was president of the Folk-Lore Society in 1953-5) than from a study of cases published by the SPR. She comments on the prevalence of reports of apparitions in countries with a moist climate; this is also the subject of comment by some of my correspondents. I believe that many of these so-called ghosts, particularly those seen in dim light, are mist figures, endowed by the onlooker with features and clothes. In countries where mist is common it is understandable that there are more reports of such figures than in a dry climate.

I referred Dr Murray's statement: ' In the dry climate of Egypt and in the desert lands there is, as far as I know, no record, ancient or modern, of such apparitions,' to Sir George Joy, a former honorary secretary of the SPR, for comment. Sir George, who was resident adviser to the sultans in the Hadhramaut States of Southern Arabia in 1940 and afterwards held posts in Aden, replied:

I cannot subscribe to the theory of Dr Murray that a moist or a dry climate has anything whatever to do with the frequency of apparitions, whatever they may be called. I have served in extremes of moist climates and dry climates in Southern Arabia and I have found no evidence of this suggestion. There are just as many alleged phantoms in the Middle East as elsewhere, and the belief in such visitations is a good deal stronger than in Western countries. ' Spirits ' might be a better word. The Arab and the Oriental will talk to the spirits of his ancestors; nor, by and large, do they scare him.

An example of an apparition seen in a dry climate is given by Mrs Violet Dickson in her book *Forty Years in Kuwait*

(George Allen and Unwin 1971). In 1928 her husband, the late Colonel H. R. P. Dickson, was appointed secretary to the Political Resident in the Persian Gulf, and judicial assistant to His Majesty's Consul-General for Fars and Khuzistan and the islands of the Persian Gulf, at Bushire, on the shores of the Arabian Gulf in Persia.

Mrs Dickson says:

One hot night when we were all sleeping on the roof I was woken up by the wind which had got up and was blowing my mosquito curtain. I sat up in bed, and there in front of me at the top of the staircase stood a figure draped in white, and wearing the Persian women's white head covering. I was too frightened to move or to wake up my husband. For a while I gazed terrified, and as I gazed the figure slowly disappeared into nothing. When I did wake Harold he did not believe I had seen anything, and insisted it was only the wind flapping the bed-sheet. But I knew I had really seen a ghost. The next morning I mentioned the incident to Ghulum Reza, our servant. 'Oh yes,' he said, 'we often see her. She was an Armenian girl who was murdered in this house.'

There is not space, in a book which is primarily an anthology, to deal with all the points raised by Dr Murray, but we have only to refer to the Cheltenham case, which I discussed in *The Unexplained* and *Apparitions and Ghosts*, for an example of a ghost seen indoors *and* outside the house. Dr Murray believes that the suddenness of the disappearance of an apparition 'suggests a current of air blowing away the particles on which it is imprinted'. May not the disappearance be due to a change in the consciousness of the person viewing the apparition?

There is some support for Dr Murray's view that apparitions appear to fade in the course of time. For example, the 'Cheltenham Ghost,' which was generally taken for a real person by those who saw it for the first time, was fainter in its later appearances in the 1880s; but as a similar figure has been seen in the neighbourhood by three men in modern times it has obviously not faded out. I am not convinced that there is any true comparison to be drawn between fading apparitions and fading photographs. Flowers also fade, as do the colours in many textiles. The list could be extended.

There is a little evidence that an electrical condition sometimes accompanies the appearance of an apparition. For instance, in the famous Versailles case the Crooke family mentioned 'a curious hissing sound that sometimes came when things were about to appear, possibly suggesting some electrical condition'; and they also spoke of a vibration in the air that accompanied vision. On 21 May 1955 a London solicitor and his wife saw in the park at Versailles the apparitions of two men and a woman; the weather then was 'very close and oppressive after a heavy thunderstorm'. But such experiences – that is, of seeing an apparition when there are electrical disturbances – are the exception rather than the rule, and we should not fall into the trap of regarding electricity as an overall explanation for what we do not understand.

It may be argued that there is 'something in the air' which causes people to experience apparitions at certain spots, such as Versailles; but, in my opinion, what influence there is to be tapped by people of suitable sensitivity is attached more to the surroundings than the air. We should be grateful to Dr Murray for raising so many lively points for discussion.

3

A Ghost Seen in a Mirror

PAMELA FRANKAU

I was only ten when I saw my first ghost, at the school called 'Claremont' in Eastbourne. It happened in broad daylight. It couldn't, I knew, be anything but a ghost; it was very frightening and it disobeyed one of the Queensberry rules for phantoms by reflecting itself in a looking glass.

The glass was on the door of a cupboard. The cupboard stood on the landing at the top of the stairs. As I came up the stairs, the cupboard door stood ajar and the door of my bedroom was wide open. The angled glass reflected a part of the room. I looked at the reflection: it showed somebody coming across the bedroom floor.

I had time to be puzzled. I shared the room with my sister and one other child; surely I had just left them both in the garden? I had time to think 'Who's this?' before it ran out of the bedroom door to meet me: a humped white shape, like a dwarf. It scuttled straight to the middle of the landing and then it wasn't there.

No light effect, no shadow, could account for it. It was a solid thing, seen first in the glass, then coming between me and the glass. There was no need to urge myself not to tell. I knew I wouldn't tell. Nor did I, until after I was grown up.

This account is taken from Miss Frankau's book *Pen to Paper* (Heinemann 1961). Miss Frankau, novelist, journalist and short-story writer, and daughter of the well-known novelist Gilbert Frankau, died in 1967, aged fifty-nine.

Miss Frankau thought that the ghost 'disobeyed one the Queensberry rules for phantoms by reflecting itself in a looking glass', but there are no Queensberry rules for apparitions, although a pattern may be discerned in these appearances, as readers of my books will know. Take, for instance, the story of the four Miss Du Canes, all sisters, related by G. N. M. Tyrrell in *Apparitions* (Duckworth 1943) as an example of an apparition seen in a mirror.

One night when they were on their way to bed, Miss Louisa Du Cane entered her bedroom, accompanied by one of her sisters and crossed to the mantelpiece at the further side to find a box of matches. The two remaining sisters also entered the room and stopped half-way across it.

There was no light [said Miss Louisa Du Cane] beyond that which glimmered through the Venetian blinds in each room. As I stood by the mantelpiece I was awe-struck by the sudden appearance of a figure gliding noiselessly towards me from the outer room. The appearance was that of a young man, of middle height, dressed in dark clothes and wearing a peaked cap. His face was very pale, and his eyes downcast as though in deep thought. His mouth was shaded by a dark moustache. The face was slightly luminous, which enabled us to distinguish the features distinctly, although we were without a light of any kind at the time.

The apparition glided onwards towards my sisters, who were standing inside the room, quite close to the outer door, and who had first caught sight of it reflected in the mirror. When within a few inches from them it vanished as suddenly as it had appeared. As the figure passed we distinctly felt a cold air which seemed to accompany it.

The Misses Du Cane furnished with their account of the experience a diagram, and Tyrrell comments that it was evident from the diagram that the two sisters would have seen the figure reflected in the mirror before they saw it directly.

Tyrrell also tells how a Lady B. and her daughter Miss B. saw an apparition reflected in a mirror. They lived in a house in which strange sounds had been heard. One night, when both ladies were sleeping in the same room, they :

. . . suddenly started up wide awake without any apparent cause, and saw a figure, in a white garment which might have been a night-dress, with dark, curly hair. . . . The room was not quite dark, although there was no artificial light except from the gas lamp in the square. No fear or any physical sensation was experienced. The figure was standing in front of the fireplace, over which there was a mirror. The position was such as to show the figure in quarter profile, and to intercept its own reflection from the mirror. It was a female figure, with hair down the back. The face, so far as was shown, was clearly visible. The two ladies both sprang out of bed to the door, which they found locked. On turning round again, the figure had disappeared.

This was Lady B.'s account. Miss B. in her statement said that she 'saw the back of the figure and its long dark hair, but not the face. The face was, however, clearly reflected in the mirror . . .'

The apparition in the next case was that of a living person who, however, died a fortnight later.

The percipient said :

I stood before the mirror doing my hair when I suddenly saw him coming from behind, as if approaching on tip-toe. His hands were outstretched, and I had an impression that he would place them on my shoulders; I could even hear his last step, like the squeak of a boot as he put his foot down. I turned in surprise, and faced him, consequently seeing him out of the glass and in the glass. As I turned I exclaimed, ' Is that you?' At least I felt that I had said that, but as I spoke he vanished.

Dr Katherine M. Briggs, past president of the Folk-Lore Society, points out in the section on ghosts in volume two of *A Dictionary of British Folk Tales* (Routledge 1971) that the motif of a ghost seen in a mirror, though otherwise invisible, is fairly widely distributed. One of her informants, the late Miss Katharine McCutcheon, told her that a house in St Leonard's School, St Andrews, was haunted by a ghost that could only be seen in a mirror. The late Stanley Lupino, a well-known actor and member of a famous stage family, also once saw a ghost reflected in a mirror, in his dressing room at Drury Lane Theatre, London. He tells this story in his autobiography *From the Stocks to the Stars* (Hutchinson 1934):

My visitor came when all the lights were on and the noise could be heard, from the street, of the people outside my window waiting to be let into the theatre. I was making-up and quite unprepared for what happened. As I was looking in the glass, I suddenly saw another face appear above mine. It was looking at me with a smile, and was also in make-up. There was a line across the forehead where a wig had been removed.

There was no mistaking that face. I had seen it many times in photographs and paintings. There was no doubt in my mind as I gazed at that reflection *that I was looking into the face of Dan Leno!*

Naturally I thought it was someone having a big joke at my expense.

I winked. The face winked back.

Then I swung round. The room was empty.

I was alert for any sound. There were the noises – of laughs, voices and traffic – from the street, but in the room all was perfectly quiet. My eyes had instinctively sought the door. There was no sign of any movement, of any abrupt exit. It was shut.

Mr Lupino thought that what he had seen was caused by some accident of light or movement of the mirror. He placed the glass at all angles and tried all kinds of experiments, but to no avail: there was no reappearance of the face. Later he learned that the room had been a favourite one of the great comedian and the last one in which he had dressed for the stage.

In his autobiography *Left Hand, Right Hand!*; extracts from which are given later in this book, Sir Osbert Sitwell, referring to this incident, said: 'I find the appearance of his [Dan Leno's] ghost to the late Stanley Lupino – which he describes in his excellent book of memoirs – most credible', and: 'In reading this story we must remember, too, how intense had been Dan Leno's sentiment for Drury Lane and his desire to appear on its boards.'

In his autobiography *Goodbye to All That* (Penguin Modern Classic, 1960) the poet Robert Graves, who served in France with the Royal Welsh Fusiliers during the First World War, tells how he stayed at Maesyneuardd, a big Tudor house near Harlech, which was 'the most haunted house that I have ever been in, though the ghosts, with one exception, were not visible, except occasionally in the mirrors'. The visible ghost, he said, 'was a little yellow dog that would appear on the lawn in the early morning to announce deaths. Nancy [his first wife, daughter of the late Sir William Nicholson] saw it through the window that time.'

An example of an apparition of the living being seen in a mirror was given to me by a correspondent, Mrs Lois M. Judd, of London. In late March/early April 1969 she was staying with her mother in an hotel in Tenerife. One night she woke and saw her mother leaning on the window with her arms folded, looking out to sea. When she called to her she did not answer, and investigation proved that her mother was at that time asleep in bed in the same room.

A few nights later I had a very similar experience, but this time my 'mother' was standing in front of the long mirror (which was on the opposite wall to her bed, and slightly on the left), combing her hair, just as she always combs her hair; what I mean is that there was nothing unusual about it, except perhaps that it was the middle of the night. She was dressed the same as before (dressing gown over her pyjamas). This time she moved (the action of combing her hair), and I could actually see her reflection in the mirror. Again I called to her and received no response. I think I must have realized what was happening, and looked over to her bed, but I don't remember whether or not I got out of bed to see. I think the vision was still there when I went back to sleep, but I cannot say for sure. Again I was not at all frightened, and again I told my mother the following morning. Although my memory fails me on some points, even after such a short space of time, I have no doubts whatsoever that I was completely awake when I saw what I call my 'hallucinations'. I am also sure that I was not dreaming about my mother before I woke. . . .

Let us now return to Miss Frankau's book. She said: 'I was only ten when I saw my first ghost.' This suggests that she had seen others. On page 104 of *Pen to Paper* she said:

I am still fascinated by ghosts, and have met many. My profession doesn't send me ghost-hunting every day. But on reflection I think that the novelist must be always something of a ghost-hunter. The mind of every human being is haunted ground and the writer's imagination leads him on; not as a member of the Psychical Research Society, explicitly studying phenomena: he is drawn into the human mysteries without being consciously aware of the process. He doesn't have to act Hawk Eye the detective, either. His explorations are the automatic work of his type of mind.

At this point the disappointed reader may say, 'Oh, was it all in her mind and didn't she really have that experience as a schoolgirl of ten?'

However, Miss Frankau draws a distinction between her 'ghosts' and what she calls 'the one real apparition'. Let us reconsider her experience. I am puzzled about the 'humped white shape, like a dwarf' which she describes. Was it, in the true sense, a figure in the shape of a human being? There is no doubt that she saw something. As she said, 'No light effect, no shadow, could account for it. It was a solid thing. . . .'

But what was it?

4

The Ghosts of India

JOHN MASTERS

The ghosts most terrible to British and Indian alike were the agonized spirits of Englishmen or women or children murdered during the Mutiny of 1857. The Central Provinces, the Bombay and Madras Presidencies and the United Provinces were dotted with towns that had once held military cantonments. Even before the Mutiny the old strong-built bungalows must have looked lonely in their compounds, as if looking for lost children and buried sons, for nearby are the cemeteries of the British dead. . . . After the Mutiny the weight of the army swung north-west into the Punjab, to the new frontiers of British power. The old cantonments perished; creepers grew up inside the bungalows; the cemeteries lay silent in the hot, unbreathing embrace of death. If there were any ghosts in such places they were as lonely as the cobras and bats who were their only companions.

But some places, such as Meerut, Delhi and Bareilly, were equally important before and after 1857. In them many of the pre-Mutiny bungalows were still inhabited and had their ghosts, and in the country around them each traveller's bungalow had its restless spirit of a woman murdered while flying from the scourge.

I had a friend, an officer of Indian cavalry, who had lived in one of these old bungalows. Something woke him one June night from a light sleep. It was very hot, and the room was airless and oppressive, but he could hear no sound. An irregular flickering light played on the wall above his bed, as though a big fire was burning on the lawn. He got up and looked, but there was no fire outside. For ten minutes more the reflected flames crawled on his wall, and then they died. The next night the firelight crawled again on his wall, and the next. The fourth night the flames were stronger, and as he could not sleep he went out on the veranda for a smoke. He thought he saw two strangely dressed figures moving across the parched grass of the lawn. He thought both figures were armed, but when he went down to look there was nothing.

The flames did not come again, but he did find out that his big garden had once contained another bungalow besides his own. On a June night in 1857 two troopers of the Bengal Native Cavalry regiment then occupying the lines had crept across the lawn and murdered their adjutant in bed there. It was the signal for the beginning of the Mutiny in that place, and an hour later the mutineers burned the bungalow to the ground as a funeral pyre for the bodies of the adjutant and his wife and two children.

There was a ghost in Lansdowne too. Lansdowne was a small cantonment town in the foothills of Garhwal and there, one night in 1937, the *havildar* commanding the quarterguard of a Frontier Force battalion noted in his log that his guard turned out at 2.20 a.m. to Grand Rounds. The field officer of the week had not made Grand Rounds that night. The *havildar*, on being questioned, explained that they had turned out to an officer with a pale face and heavy whiskers, wearing white mess dress uniform. He had ridden up in the darkness on a grey horse and had not said a word except to answer the sentry's challenge with the usual phrase, 'Grand Rounds'. The guard had turned out to the Lansdowne ghost, who appeared every ten years or so and was occasionally seen at a distance, riding slowly, head down in the moonlight, along a bridle path under overhanging trees. He was said to be a man who lost his wife in the Mutiny, and after a year's lonely brooding, shot himself in Lansdowne.

This extract is taken from *Bugles and a Tiger* by John Masters

(Michael Joseph 1956). It relates to the time when he was an officer in the Indian Army in the 1930s.

The experience of the officer of Indian cavalry who saw the reflection of the fires that came from the direction of his lawn where a bungalow had once stood presumably involved retrocognition.

Sir Ernest Bennett's book *Apparitions and Haunted Houses* (Faber 1939) contains an account of the phantom figure of an officer on horseback seen at the hill station of Murree in the Punjab, and this is particularly interesting because Murree is only a few hundred miles from Garhwal.

The account was sent to the SPR in 1888 by Major-General R. Barter, of Careystown, Whitegate, County Cork. He said that in 1854, when he was a subaltern in the 75th Regiment, he rented a house at Murree called Uncle Tom's Cabin. This house had been built a year or two before by a Lieutenant B. who had died at Peshawur on 2 January 1854.

Lieutenant Barter, as he was then, had just said good-bye to some guests near his house. He was about to return home when he heard the ring of a horse's hoof as the shoe struck the stones of a bridle path that led to his house. Presently he saw a tall hat appear, evidently worn by the rider of the animal. The steps came nearer, and in a few seconds round the corner appeared a man mounted on a pony with two *syces* or grooms.

The moon was at the full, a tropical moon, 'so bright that you could see to read a newspaper by its light,' the officer said. They were above him by some eight to ten feet on the bridle path. The rider was in full dinner dress, with white waistcoat, and wearing a tall chimney-pot hat, and he sat on a powerful dark-brown hill pony in a listless sort of way, the reins hanging loosely from both hands. A *syce* led the pony at each side.

Lieutenant Barter challenged the party. 'Instantly the group came to a halt, the rider gathering the bridle reins up with both hands, turned his face, which had hitherto been looking away from me, towards me and looked down upon me. The group was still as in a tableau, with the bright moon shining full upon it, and I at once recognized the rider as Lieutenant B., whom I had formerly known. The face, however, was different from what it used to be; in place of being clean-shaven as when I knew it, it was now surrounded by a fringe (what used to be known as a Newgate fringe), and it was the face of a dead man, the ghastly waxen pallor of it brought out more distinctly in the moonlight by the fringe of dark hair by which it was encircled; the body, too, was far stouter than when I had known it in life.

'I marked all this in a moment, and then resolved to lay hold of the thing whatever it was. I dashed up the bank, and the earth which had been thrown on the side giving under my feet I fell forward up the bank on my hands; recovering myself instantly, I gained the road, and stood in the exact spot where the group had been, but which was now vacant; there wasn't a trace of anything. . . .'

The following day Lieutenant Barter talked to a fellow officer who had known Lieutenant B. up to the time of his death and discovered that he had become very stout and had grown a fringe on his sick bed. The officer recognized the pony from Lieutenant Barter's description of it and said that Lieutenant B. had killed the animal when riding down a hill in a reckless fashion.

In the remaining six weeks when they were in Uncle Tom's Cabin Lieutenant Barter and his wife repeatedly heard the sound of a man riding rapidly down the path to the house but the apparition was not seen again.

Mrs Barter confirmed that she had heard the sound of a horse being galloped down the path 'and round our house, at break-neck speed, the panting of the horse being quite audible'.

I believe it is possible that this tale of a phantom officer on horseback circulated in the district and gave rise to the accounts of the appearances of the Lansdowne ghost.

Another account of soldiers on sentry duty who saw an apparition, this time that of a nurse, was sent to me some years ago. It is published here for the first time. The report came from Mr H. Pierce, of Wycombe Marsh, Buckinghamshire, who in 1921, when he was nineteen years old, was serving with the 98th Battery RFA, 1st Field Brigade, at Clonmel, County Tipperary.

He said that with a soldier named Dunn he was on sentry duty at the barracks between midnight and 2 a.m. They were standing in an archway when they heard their relief coming. As my correspondent issued a challenge to the relieving patrol in the usual way he heard Dunn also issue a challenge. He turned and saw a young nurse pass by the archway, coming from the direction of the hospital. 'We could hear the pitter-patter of her feet as she hurried along the roadway, and the white veil that nurses wear on their heads was fluttering in the breeze as she went along,' he said. As Dunn issued the second challenge, 'Halt or I'll fire,' the nurse turned left at the end of the barrack block and the magazine into a cul-de-sac where there was much barbed wire. The two soldiers were joined by the sergeant in charge of the guard and two other men. When they investigated there was no sign of the 'nurse'.

My correspondent said he was told in a nearby public house that this 'nurse' had been seen several times before. The apparition was said to be that of a nurse who was in love with a young officer. They used to meet in a tunnel that started where the sentries saw her turn left but one evening she was killed when the tunnel collapsed. The officer was not with her at the time as he had overslept.

Presumably this occurrence reported by Mr Pierce would be included in the log the guard commander, Sergeant Manning.

If any reader has information about the apparition of the nurse at Clonmel or about the Lansdowne ghost I shall be glad to hear from him.

5

The Boy with the Flowers

NGAIO MARSH

My mother possessed a faculty which, if she had been a Highlander, would have been called the second-sight. Can it, I ask myself, have stemmed from that great uncle with Scottish estates who so disastrously expired in his family chaise? She was not at all proud of this attribute and generally preferred to ignore it, but occasionally it manifested itself with such inconsequent emphasis that we were obliged to take notice of it. I shall give three instances of her powers, if powers they were.

It may be remembered that in my earliest childhood [in New Zealand] we were visited by my father's 'wild' brother, tubercular Uncle Reggie. He returned to England in due course. Some considerable time afterwards my mother in the small hours of the night roused my father with the strange remark that 'Reggie is about and I think he wants us'. My father reassured her and himself returned to unconsciousness. My mother, however . . . rose from her bed, lit her candle, took a pencil, consulted her clock and tore the current leaflet from the day-to-day calendar that stood on her dressing-table. Having written the exact time upon this leaflet, she folded it, tucked it behind the bulk of the calendar, returned to bed and to sleep and, in due course, forgot the incident. She remembered it some weeks later when my grandmother wrote from England that at that very hour, sitting in a garden chair in the heat of the day, Uncle Reggie had incontinently expired.

The second example of her prescience occurred when I was teaching the small boy Colin [the son of one of New Zealand's most distinguished surgeons], to whom I was very much attached. His parents had taken a cottage near us for the holidays and Colin was in the habit of paying us a morning visit, often bringing me one of those warm knots of decapitated geraniums which children like to present. My mother was engaged, with my help, in the annual task of dusting and rearranging the books which we accumulated in great numbers. She was gently, if reprehensibly, slapping two of them together on the veranda when she remarked that Colin was coming up the garden path and that he had his usual bunch of geraniums and wore a smart new Norfolk jacket. She asked me to meet him and keep him out of doors as she was busy. I went down one path and up another. I called. I explored the gully. He was nowhere to be seen. 'Funny little boy,' said my mother, slapping her books. 'He must have gone home again'.

The next morning he arrived saying that he had intended to come the previous day but had been a naughty boy and his nanny had forbidden him. 'And', he said, 'I'd got my new coat on and I'd picked you a bunch of geraniums'.

These two incidents can, I suppose, be explained on assumption of thought transference. Both Uncle Reggie, in his extremity, and Colin, in his childish frustration, might be held to have set up some kind of telepathic communication. The third event is difficult to rationalize.

It also concerns a small boy – a cousin called Beynham Pyne. My mother, during her afternoon siesta, looked up from her book and saw a bed in a strong light with a little boy in it. He turned his head and smiled. She wondered which of her nephews this might be and, as was her habit with these occurrences, dismissed the matter from her mind. Some weeks later my Aunt Madeline sent a message to say Beynham was to have his tonsils removed. She asked my mother to sustain her during the operation which was to be performed in the house. When my mother arrived they went into the sick room and she thought: this will be what I saw. But it was all wrong. The bed was in the wrong place, the light was coming from the wrong direction. Beynham did not turn his head. She thought: so much for *that*. She and my aunt went into another room and presently the nurse came to say the operation was successfully over and they could come and see the patient.

When they re-entered the room the bed had been moved into a bay window and there was a better light. Beynham turned his head and smiled at them.

The above extracts are taken from Dame Ngaio's autobiography *Black Beech and Honeydew*, published by Collins in 1966.

The first example given by the distinguished New Zealand-born novelist and detective story writer is a typical example of a crisis case. Her mother was aware that Reggie 'was about'; she must have had a sense of his presence, although he was physically twelve thousand miles away, but she did not, apparently 'see' him. My first inclination was to treat the case of the boy Colin as one of false arrival, but as he did not arrive in his new coat until the following morning this may be regarded as an example of precognition, although rather an inconsequential one. The same remark may be made about the case of Beynham Pyne. It is interesting that the writer's mother should have had her vision of the boy in a bed in a strong light while she was reading. I have commented in *Apparitions and Ghosts* on the number of people who had psychical experiences while reading. As Dr R. H. Thouless, the well-known psychologist, remarked when I referred this point to him, 'It seems to suggest that detachment of attention from the immediate problems of adapting to the external world may be a favourable condition for a *psi*-experience.'[1]

[1] Dr Louisa E. Rhine, the American parapsychologist, points out in *ESP in Life and Lab* (Collier-Macmillan 1967) that for decades the term *psi* has been used in parapsychology whenever it is desirable to describe phenomena of the entire field of the paranormal.

6

Faces in the Wind

W. H. HUDSON

One autumn evening some years ago I was walking home in a London street, walking briskly in the face of a strong southwest wind, the one I love best of all winds in this hemisphere, thinking of nothing except that I was thirsty for my tea and that the wind was very delightful, when something extraordinary occurred, something never hitherto experienced. This was the appearance of a face – the face of a girl well known and very dear to me, who lived at that time at home with her people at a distance of eighty miles from where I was. It was the face only, the vivid image of the face, so vividly seen that it could not have appeared a more real human face if the girl had actually come before me. But, as I said, only the face, and it appeared to be in and a part of the wind, since it did not rest still for one instant, but had a flutter like the flutter we used to see in a cinematograph picture, and continually moved to and fro and vanished and reappeared almost every second, always keeping on a level with and about three feet removed from my eyes. The flutter and motion generally was like that of a flag or of some filmy substance agitated by the wind. Then it vanished and I saw it no more.

It was to me an amazing experience, as I am about the last person in the universe to suffer from delusions and illusions, being, as someone has said, 'too disgustingly sane for anything', or at all events to experience such things; and I consequently soon came to the conclusion that this phantom was of a nature of a telepathic communication. Whether or not it was a right conclusion, the reader will judge when he knows the sequel. But I must first relate a second similar experience which came to me two years later.

I was out in a high wind, an exceptionally violent and very cold east wind in early March, on this occasion blowing on my back, and I was walking very fast over a heath towards a huge pile of rocks forming a headland on the west Cornish coast. I had visited the headland on the previous day, and had sat a long time on the summit of the rocky pile watching the sea birds, and on coming home I discovered to my disgust that I had left my nice thick leather gloves on the rock where I had pulled them off. And this high rock was unfortunately the favourite resort of a pair of ravens. My object now was to look for my gloves, with little hope that the ravens had not succeeded in tearing them to pieces in trying to devour them, or simply because of their innate cussedness.

This, simply, was the sole subject occupying my mind, when suddenly once more I had the strange experience of a face fluttering before me – just a face as on the former occasion, just as real in appearance, at the same distance from my eyes, fluttering, moving as if blown to and fro, appearing and disappearing as before.

It was the face of a lady, an intimate and dear friend who was at a distance of something under four hundred miles from me at that moment.

As in the former case, I concluded that it was a telepathic message, and in that belief I rest. Why this phantasm appeared to me at that moment I am not at liberty to tell, but there is now unhappily no reason for the same reticence with regard to the first case; death has prematurely removed the dear souls who were the principal actors in that little drama, and its relating can hurt no one.

It was the case of a girl of fourteen I loved as much as if she had been my own daughter, because of her sweetness and charm and loving disposition, the bright clear temper of her mind and other engaging qualities; and I wished to adopt her – a desire or craving that sometimes attacks a childless man. She too desired it, but there were difficulties in the way which could not be overcome, and so that matter was dropped, or rather left for the time in abeyance. The appearance of that phantasmal face caused me to write at once to the mother to inquire after them all, particularly my favourite girl, and her reply was that they were all well and going on as usual, etc. Somehow this did not quite satisfy me; something in the child's mind had caused that vision, although the mother was perhaps ignorant of it. Before long I was able to pay them a visit, and found them, as I had been told, all well and going on as usual. The girl told me nothing, and I asked no questions. Nevertheless a suspicion lurked in my mind, and presently I became conscious of a slight change in the moral or mental atmosphere of the place, a change so slight that it could not be described as a restraint or a chill, but it was there all the same, a something which had come to dim the old bright family happiness and union.

[Hudson goes on to describe that the family was 'intensely religious' and the parents had felt that it was necessary for all to undergo 'conversion' as part of their Evangelistic faith. This they had done except for the girl of whom Hudson was fond.]

She went to church and said her prayers, and thought that was enough. But I did not know, for this she kept from me, that the pressure which had been brought to bear on her had become increasingly painful until the breaking point was reached.

About that I now heard. On the second day of my visit the mother, finding me alone, said there was something she thought it right to tell me. I had written to her a little while back, inquiring, as she thought, a little anxiously about their welfare, especially about my young friend, and she had answered that they were all well. So they were, but a day or two before receiving my letter there had been an exceedingly painful scene with the girl. She had suddenly, to their amazement, broken out in a passionate revolt against them on account of the religious question which had been troubling their minds. She told them that she had prayed to Heaven to send me to her assistance – to protect and deliver her from them. She had also, she said, made up her mind to leave them, and if she had no money to pay the railway fare, she would walk and live on charity by the way until she came to where I was or she found me. It was, the mother said, a trying situation, and gave them all the greatest pain; they began to think they had worried her too much about her religious indifference. They told her how sorry they were, and succeeded in pacifying her by promising not to trouble her any more, but to leave her to follow her own mind about such matters.

They must indeed have gone through a painful experience, I thought, seeing the state of mind it had caused in the mother, which made her open her heart to me about it, knowing, too, beforehand on which side my sympathies would lie.

Believers in telepathy will say that I was justified in my belief that there could be no explanation of my strange experience other than the one given; while the unbeliever will say, as usual, that it was nothing but coincidence.

My experience – the two appearances of phantasmal faces – has been described here solely because it somehow appears to fit in with my whole idea about the wind – its powerful effect on the mind, or shall we say on the matter or substance of the mind; and I do not find it impossible to believe that one of its effects is to make the mind more sensitive to telepathic communications. In both instances the wind, a strong south-west wind and an east wind blowing a gale, blew from the direction of the persons whose minds were occupied with me at that time.

Perhaps I should have seen the faces if the wind had been blowing in other directions. I doubt it. As I have said, they appeared to be in the wind, and of it, as if the wind had blown them like gossamer or thistledown to me. Doubtless, they were images on the brain, projected into the air, as it seemed, and their incessant windy motions perhaps corresponded with an agitation in the brain, or with that substance of it in which the affections, memory, reason and imagination reside, with perhaps other faculties we know not of or are only just beginning to know. And if, as I imagine, the wind was the cause of the agitation of the brain – the wind or the subtle immaterial substance which pervades the brain and the winds alike, or perhaps moves with the wind – then the direction in which it blows may be a fact to be taken into account as wafting or blurring or making a vivid mental message from a distance.

This extract is taken from Hudson's last book, *A Hind in Richmond Park*, published by Dent in 1922, the year of his death. A bird sanctuary with decorative work by Jacob Epstein was opened in Hyde Park, London, as a memorial to the great naturalist in 1925. Hudson was particularly sensitive to the effects of wind and was a firm believer in telepathy. It is probably true, as he believed, that the wind in certain circumstances increased his sensitivity, but I feel I cannot agree with him when he thinks it significant that in these two experiences the wind was blowing from the direction of the person of whom he was fond. I believe that telepathy is a mental process, not a physical one. Also, distance is not a significant factor in telepathy. To sum up: Hudson had such a great love of the wind that he twice saw in it the faces of women whom he loved. It may be asked, 'Why only faces? Why not the whole figure?' We do not know the answer to this question, but we do know that many cases have been recorded in which only part of a figure was seen.

7

The Guardian of the Treasure

MAURICE COLLIS

I myself had once seen a guardian ghost. [Maurice Collis recalls this as he returns home to his house on the banks of the Irrawaddy after watching a so-called necromancer digging for treasure after securing the ghost which guarded it]. I was in Arakan at the time, the north-western seaboard of Burma, and was spending the night in the deserted capital of the Arakanese kings. The rest-house was on the reputed site of their treasury. It was a wooden structure raised on piles, with a wide flight of steps leading up to the veranda. I was seated in a room off the veranda and by the light of an oil lamp could see the steps. Mr San Shwe Bu, the Arakanese archaeologist, was talking to me. At about nine o-clock I felt the building quiver and sway for a moment. My companion looked up in surprise. 'Like a little earthquake,' he said.

At that instant I dimly saw an old Arakanese woman slowly mounting the steps. It was much too late for anyone to come with a petition and I stared at the woman in some surprise, while she stared back at me from the top step with an intent expression on her wrinkled face. For an appreciable time she regarded me so and then passed from sight, as if down the veranda, from which there was no exit except into the rooms.

'Somebody's outside,' I exclaimed, jumping up, but I knew that I had seen a ghost, for there is no confusing a ghost with a mortal. It is not your eyes that tell you, but a sense that leaps up suddenly within. We went on to the veranda and searched the rooms. There was nobody there, nor did I expect to find anyone.

Next morning, when some local notabilities came to pay me a call, I said something about it. They looked at me with interest and increased respect. 'Your Honour saw the female ghost bound to this spot by the old kings to guard their treasure,' they explained. 'She is seen mounting the steps and always passes down the veranda.'

'How did the kings bind a spirit?' I asked.

'They buried a person alive at the proper place.'

'Yes, yes, but why should that bind the spirit?'

'At the moment of death the spirit was caught in a magical net.'

'I do not understand.'

'Our old kings understood, as your Honour has seen for yourself.'

'Why did the house shake first?'

'The ghost desired to attract your Honour's attention.'

'How did she shake the house?'

It was not the house she shook, but your Honour's mind.'

At the time of this incident (1928) Mr Collis was Deputy Commissioner in charge of the administration of the Sagaing district in the heart of Upper Burma. He relates it in *Trials in Burma* (Faber 1938). Although the local notabilities ascribed the 'shaking' of the building to an activity of the ghost which affected the writer's mind – in other words, to a psychological process – we must remember that Collis's companion also felt the building quiver and remarked that it was 'like a little earthquake'. My conclusion from this is that the movement of the building was due to some physical cause. The rest-house was a wooden structure raised on piles and it would not take much movement of the earth to cause such a building to quiver. I have lived in buildings in Burma similar to those described by

Collis and remember them as frail structures. However, the movement of a building should not have had the effect of making him see an apparition immediately afterwards. It would have been different if a series of disturbances over a long period had affected his nerves, but such circumstances did not apply in this case. The writer's remark that 'there is no confusing a ghost with a mortal. It is not your eyes that tell you, but a sense which leaps up suddenly within', is worth noting as an example of psychological insight. It is also worth noting that legends about ghosts that guard treasure are found in many parts of the world.

8

Pictures in the Crystal

ALICE POLLOCK

I have had many psychic experiences during my life. . . . My mother had a 'sixth sense' and was sometimes forewarned of things that were to happen. All my sisters had a certain amount of psychic power, but none of them developed it to the extent that I did. Eleanor was the one who was most interested and encouraged me to use my power; it was she who gave me my first crystal, and she introduced me to people who wanted help either in foreseeing the future or in uncovering the past of a house or property by psychometry. These introductions often led to the most unexpected adventures.

One blazing hot day, when it was really too hot to do anything, I had promised Eleanor that I would spend the afternoon with her, and so I had to keep my promise.

When I arrived she said : 'I am anxious for you to psychometrize a letter from Norman for me.' Norman was her daughter-in-law. Then she quickly added : 'I want to know if they are going to move house, also if she is going to have another child.'

I was really annoyed with her; she knew quite well that I particularly disliked knowing who a letter was from or to be asked to answer any particular question. I always maintained that I had to make my mind a blank so as to receive whatever came, and if I was told who the letter was from and asked to answer a lot of questions, it was confusing and made everything difficult.

However, I took the letter and stood in the middle of the

room, as I disliked coming into contact with any furniture while psychometrizing. The sun was shining in the room, and it was hot, but I preferred the daylight and would not have the curtains drawn.

I had hardly got the letter in my hand when I felt very ill. I became worse. I went very cold and could feel nothing in my arms and side. I said: 'There is a man who is very ill, paralysed down his left side. The condition is caused by injury to the spine: he is with relations who think he will recover, but he will die quite soon.'

By this time my looks had frightened Eleanor and she took the letter out of my hands and rubbed my arm until I could feel it again, I sat quiet for a time, and then feeling much better, I said: 'Is there anything in the letter about illness?' and she said: 'No, it is about the grandchildren.'

'Look again and see if you have misssed anything.'

She read the letter through and she had omitted to notice a P.S. on the back of the last sheet. It said: 'I have just heard from Mrs B. that her son is ill.'

Mrs B.'s son was a friend of Eleanor's son, who had died in the war, but Eleanor did not know him well.

No more was said at the time, but three days later Eleanor had a letter from her daughter-in-law, saying: 'I have heard from Mrs B. Her son is paralysed down the left side. It is caused by spine trouble, but he is getting on well and they have every hope of his recovery.

He was dead in a fortnight.

My cousin, Cornwallis Wykeham-Martin, once asked me to psychometrize one of the rooms at Leeds Castle [Mrs Pollock's father was the third son of Mr Charles and Lady Jemima Wykeham-Martin of Leeds Castle, Kent]. I assented readily and he chose for the experiment a room in the old Castle called Henry VIII's room. It was the room my parents always occupied when they stayed there. I went alone into the room, and had been there some time without any result. Then suddenly the room changed: it was no longer the comfortably furnished, rather modern room, but was cold and bare, with little furniture and no carpet. There was a large fireplace, not in the situation of the present one, with logs burning on the hearth. Then I saw a tall woman wearing a long, flowing white robe, her hair hanging loose, pacing up and down the length of the room, wringing her hands and evidently in great distress.

Cornwallis was interested. He told me that at one time Queen Joan of Navarre, stepmother of Henry v, had been imprisoned in that room for a few days on her way to Pevensey, and thence to France. And now I quote from my grandfather's book: 'The Queen was accused of witchcraft and of trying by this means to kill her stepson, the King. She was despoiled of all her goods, beds, etc., and given a small allowance until shortly before Henry's death, when apparently his conscience smote him and he ordered all her moneys and goods to be restored to her. She came back to Leeds Castle and stayed there until she went to Havering-atte-Bower, where she lived till she died, 1437'.

Eleanor took me to tea with her friend, Lady Thomson, who was interested in psychic matters and for this reason was anxious to make my acquaintance.

We had tea and after discussing psychic phenomena in a general way, Lady Thomson said, 'I have just bought a cottage in Buckinghamshire. Can you tell me if it will be lucky for me?'

I said I did not see how I could possibly psychometrize the cottage without going to it, or at any rate having something tangible to hold. Then I asked, 'Could you draw me a plan of the house?'

I knew she was an artist and I thought she might be able to do this. She was delighted and at once drew a plan of the downstairs rooms. There was a passage through the cottage from front to back, with a room on either side of the front door, and the kitchen and scullery at the back.

I was at once attracted to the room on the right of the front door, and said, 'It is a small room and there is a large old-fashioned fireplace where logs are burning.'

'No, that is not so,' said Lady Thomson, 'it is just an ordinary modern fireplace.'

I however, still visualized the fireplace, and then I saw a little girl, apparently very badly injured – I thought burned. She was carried by some people to the room on the other side of the front door, where she died almost immediately. I saw nothing else.

Lady Thomson was interested, and said she was going to the cottage in a day or two, and would try and find out some of its history for me.

About a week later she went down to the cottage, and when she arrived she found a great surprise awaiting her. The workmen had to replace some worn skirting boards near the fireplace in the room on the right of the front door. They had found after removing the skirting boards that there was a gap behind. They investigated and found the modern fireplace there had been built up in front of an old open fireplace like the one I had described.

This made Lady Thomson more keen than ever on finding out the history of the cottage. She asked many people, with no success, until someone suggested that an old man, who had lived all his life in the village, might remember something. Lady Thomson went at once to see him, and she told him how they had found the old fireplace, and asked him whether he knew anything about it.

'Oh, yes,' he said at once, 'there was an old open fireplace

CHICAGO HEIGHTS FREE PUBLIC LIBRARY

there many years ago, but there was a dreadful accident when a little girl was left alone in the room. She fell into the fire and was badly burned, and she died after they had moved her into the room on the other side of the passage. After this tragedy the old fireplace was built up, and a new modern grate put in.'

I had a great friend called Cissie MacRae. We met when we were both quite young; she was an ardent member of the Suffragettes. Her mother lived in the dower house on the shores of Loch Fyne in Scotland. After her mother's death, her brother begged Cissie to keep on the dower house at Ballimore. This she did, and I stayed with her nearly every year. . . .

Cissie was a wonderful friend and a great loss to me when she died. It was during one of my visits to her in Scotland that I had another psychic experience. Cissie came to me one morning with a letter. She said, ' Alice, I think this will interest you very much. It is from some friends of mine who live the other side of the county. They have been unfortunate in having to sell most of the estate and only the house and a few acres of land now remain. The family consists of two sisters and a brother, middle-aged, and with no near relations and no heir to the property. They possessed an old crystal ball which had been in the family for generations. This has suddenly and mysteriously disappeared, much to their concern. They had searched high and low and inquired among the crofters, and eventually given up all hope of finding it.

' In this letter they say the crystal has been recovered and this is how it happened. There had been a heavy storm and some of the crofters had gone down to the foreshore in the morning to see whether anything of value had been washed up. One of them saw what he thought was a piece of glass; he picked it up and examined it more closely and came to the conclusion that it was a crystal. Several people gathered round to look at his find, and one of them wondered whether it could be the crystal that the Laird set so much store by and which had so mysteriously disappeared. It was certainly worth finding out. They took it up to the house, where it was acclaimed as the heirloom, much to the delight of the owners. They ask me whether I can persuade you to try to psychometrize it.'

I had done much divination with Cissie at different times, and she had great faith in my powers and had told her friends about me. They were nervous of parting with their treasure even for a short time and sent it over by a special messenger on the understanding that they would send for it the next day. It was a curious-looking piece of crystal, about four inches in diameter, triangular in shape, rough and discoloured and cracked.

On holding it, I got the impression of some rather rough ground sloping down to the sea. There were no cliffs, only a bank, and on the bank I saw the ancient remains of a chapel. This I came to the conclusion had a great deal of history, but I could get no further with it. I then described a man whom I saw ill in a hospital bed. Cissie at once explained, 'That is Ian' (the owner of the crystal). Several nurses were in attendance, and a priest who was obviously going to officiate. I knew that he was a Roman Catholic. I also said, 'The sick man is married. He will die quite soon.' I got nothing further, and handed the crystal back to Cissie.

She said, 'The only thing that you described rightly was the coastline and the old chapel which exists on the estate. The rest of it is absolutely untrue. He is certainly not a Roman Catholic; they are strict Presbyterians. Also he is not married, much to the disappointment of his sisters.'

So that was that, and the crystal went back the following day. I heard no more about it until three months afterwards, when Cissie wrote to me, 'An extraordinary thing has happened. Everything you said about the Scotch crystal is true. The sisters had a telegram to say their brother was taken ill

in Edinburgh and would they come at once. They found him
in hospital and very ill, in fact there was little hope for his
recovery. To their utter amazement, a Roman Catholic priest
was at the bedside and administered the last rites. Their brother
told them that he had been a Roman Catholic for some time.
He died the next day, and after his death it was disclosed that
he had been secretly married for some time but there were no
children.'

Mrs Pollock was a remarkable woman and had some remarkable experiences. Her book from which these extracts are taken,
Portrait of My Victorian Youth (Johnson 1971), was written
when she was 102. She died in October 1971, aged 103. Her
daughter, Lady Anson, told me that her mother ceased using
her psychical gifts when she was between sixty and seventy
'because they took so much out of her'. At that age, however, her powers were still strong. It may be objected that when
Mrs Pollock's book was first published she was so old that her
recollection of the past could not be trusted, but this is not the
impression I gained from a close reading of the book. She is,
for instance, critical of professional fortune tellers who feel
they *must* produce results, even when they are getting little for
the sitter.

I was particularly interested in the account of the cottage
in Buckinghamshire where there was an old-fashioned fireplace
hidden by 'an ordinary modern fireplace'. Mrs Pollock did not
'see' the modern fireplace but the old-fashioned one. This
experience may be compared with that told to me by the late
Mr W. E. Manning when I was collecting material for
Apparitions and Ghosts. He said that when he was preparing
for bed one night he heard a noise 'as if iron was being knocked
against iron. I looked round and saw a man in a wine-coloured
dressing gown raking out the coals of a dying fire . . . an interesting point of this experience is that the grate had been

hidden by a gas fire for at least thirty years. If I saw the ghost of a dead man I also saw the ghost of a dead fire.'

From Mrs Pollock's account of her experience in Leeds Castle, as well as that just given about the hidden fireplace, it seems that she was able to exercise on occasions strong powers of retrocognition in which modern features of a room disappeared and were replaced by those of the past.

It is interesting that on occasions Mrs Pollock should have used a crystal. As. F. W. H. Myers pointed out in *Human Personality and its Survival of Bodily Death* (Longmans, 1903), crystal-gazing in some form has been practised for at least three thousand years and is virtually of world-wide distribution. The crystal, he said, was only one of many objects used in a similar way as a means of obtaining supernormal knowledge through induced hallucinations. Other examples are vessels containing liquid – usually water; water in springs; mirrors of polished steel; liquid poured into the palm of the hand; a drop of blood or ink; and various objects with a reflecting surface, such as the beryl or other gems, the blade of a sword, a ball of polished stone or a human finger-nail. From Mrs Pollock's account of her experience in Scotland it does not seem that she saw her vision in the crystal; rather, it was a means of inducing the vision. But often the vision is seen in the crystal; hence the heading of this chapter.

9
Vision in a Ruined Chapel
GEORGE RUSSELL (A.E.)

I waited for a friend inside a ruined chapel and while there a phantasm of its ancient uses came vividly before me. In front of the altar I saw a little crowd kneeling, most prominent a woman in a red robe, all pious and emotionally intent. A man stood behind these leaning by the wall as if too proud to kneel. An old man in ecclesiastical robes, abbot or bishop, stood, a crozier in one hand, while the other was uplifted in blessing or in emphasis of his words. Behind the cleric a boy carried a vessel, and the lad's face was vain with self-importance. I saw all this suddenly as if I was contemporary and was elder in the world by many centuries. I could surmise the emotional abandon of the red-robed lady, the proud indifference of the man who stood with his head but slightly bent, the vanity of the young boy as servitor in the ceremony, just as in a church today we feel the varied mood of those present. Anything may cause such pictures to rise in vivid illumination before us, a sentence in a book, a word, or contact with some object. . . .

It is not only rocks and ruins which infect us with such visions. A word in a book when one is sensitive may do this also. I sought in a classical dictionary for information about some myth. What else on the page caught my eye I could not say, but something there made two thousand years to vanish. I was looking at the garden of a house in some ancient city. From the house into the garden fluttered two girls, one in purple and the other in a green robe, and they, in a dance of excitement, ran to the garden wall and looked beyond it to the right. There a street rose high to a hill where there was a pillared building. I could see through blinding sunlight a crowd swaying down the street drawing nigh the house, and the two girls were as excited as girls might be today if king or queen were entering their city. This instant uprising of images following a glance at a page cannot be explained as the refashioning of the pictures of memory. The time which elasped after the page was closed and the apparition in the brain was a quarter of a minute or less. One can only surmise that pictures so vividly coloured, so full of motion and sparkles as are moving pictures in the theatres, were not an instantaneous creation by some magical artist within us, but were evoked out of a vaster memory than the personal; that the Grecian names my eye had caught had the power of symbols which evoked their affinities, and the picture of the excited girls and the shining procession was in some fashion, I know not how, connected with what I had read.

This extract is taken from A.E.'s book *The Candle of Vision* (Macmillan 1918).

Russell was a large bearded man who filled a prominent place in Irish letters, being a close friend of W. B. Yeats, another mystic. Theosophy supplied him with a framework for his instinctive beliefs. According to *The Dictionary of National Biography* (Oxford University Press 1949), Russell looked consistently to the antiquity of all races for the oracles of a universal wisdom-religion, and in Irish mythology he sought for hints of an ancestral lore identical with that of the sages of the East. He had great gifts as a painter which he never fully developed. It is as a poet that he is best remembered. Russell died at Bournemouth on 17 July 1935, aged seventy-two.

In L. A. G. Strong's *Green Memory*, extracts from which are given elsewhere in this book, Strong wrote :

Of all the men and women I have met, A.E. met life with the greatest serenity. I know that it is difficult to give reasons for so extreme a claim. The effect he made was like that of certain rare experiences of the spirit wherein one is given a glimpse of beauty or of harmony on a very deep level : its very completeness makes it impossible to describe. To describe such things is to break them up into attributes, whereas their essence lies in being indivisible.

Not that A.E. lacked attributes. He was many-sided enough to excite remark in a nation of the versatile and the quick-witted. Poet, painter, editor, journalist, mystic, economist, negotiator, he was all sorts of men; but all his attributes were facets of a single personality, and all of him went into each of them. They were like the different lenses through which the beam of a lighthouse is successively flashed on the surrounding darkness. Each carried his whole power at the moment, yet he was more than the sum of them all.

By the time I met him, on the August evening in 1924, he was a great tweed-clad, shaggy-bearded, teddy-bear of a man, beaming on the world through large glasses, speaking in a soft voice which was so soothing that now and then one jumped in surprise, realizing a second afterwards the pitch and point of what it had said. Gentleness and serenity : the space around him was full of peace, like the proverbial centre of a hurricane. All bitterness and all contention seemed to cease as soon as he came into a room. During the worst of the Troubles men could meet affably in his house who would have snarled at each other, or worse, in the street outside. He did not need a dramatic setting. Benevolence radiated from him, and it was never silly.

Russell describes how he developed 'through meditation a more powerful orientation of my being as if to a hidden sun, and my thoughts turned more and more to the spiritual life of Earth'. In one passage he said :

I will not speak here of high things because I am trying to argue with people who see no wonder in anything, and dismiss all high things with a silly phrase as fancy or imagination or hallucination.

But I know from questioning many people that it is common with them before they sleep to see faces, while their eyes are closed, and they are, as they think, alone. These faces are sometimes the faces of imps who frown at them, put out their tongues at them, grin or gibber. Sometimes not a face but a figure, or figures, will be seen which, like the faces, seems endowed with life. To call this imagination or fancy is to explain nothing because the explanation is not explained. The more one concentrates on these most trivial mental apparitions, the more certain do we feel they have a life of their own, and that our brain is as full of living creatures as our body is thronged with tiny cells, each a life, or as the blood may swarm with bacteria. I draw attention to the mystery in obvious and common things, and ask that they be explained and not slurred over as if no explanation were necessary.

Russell's visions were not only of scenes in the past. He worked for a time for a brewery company, and later in a drapery business in Dublin, and said:

Once in an idle interval in my work I sat with my face pressed in my hands, and in that dimness pictures began flickering in my brain. I saw a little dark shop, the counter before me, and behind it an old man fumbling with some papers, a man so old that his motions had lost swiftness and precision. Deeper in the store was a girl, red-haired, with grey watchful eyes fixed on the old man. I saw that to enter the shop one must take two steps downwards from a cobbled pavement without. I questioned a young man, my office companion, who then was writing a letter, and I found that what I had seen was his father's shop. All my imaginations – the old man, his yellow-white beard, his fumbling movements, the watchful girl, her colour, the steps, the cobbled pavement – were not imaginations of mine in any true sense, for while I was in a vacant mood my companion had been thinking of his home, and his brain was populous with quickened memories, and they invaded my own mind, and when I made question I found their origin. . . . The vision of the girl and the old man may in reality have been but a little part of the images with which my brain was flooded.

Did I then see all, or might not other images in the same series emerge at some later time and the connection be lost? If I had written a tale and had imagined an inner room, an old mother, an absent son, a family trouble, might I not all the while be still adventuring in another's life? While we think we are imagining a character we may, so marvellous are the hidden ways, be really interpreting a being actually existing, brought into psychic contact with us by some affinity of sentiment or soul.

In one interesting passage (on page 165) Russell says: 'I was drawn to meditate beside a deep pool amid woods. It was a place charged with psychic life, and was regarded with some awe by the people who lived near. As I gazed into the dark waters consciousness seemed to sink beneath them and I found myself in another world. It was more luminous than this. . . .' It seems that, by gazing into the pool, he had achieved a state of dissociation of personality similar to that obtained by crystal-gazing.

Another person who apparently had visions of the past was Miss Eleanor Jourdain, the second principal of St Hugh's College, Oxford, and co-author, with Miss Annie Moberly, the first principal, of that celebrated book *An Adventure*, which I have discussed in earlier volumes.

Mrs Lucille Iremonger, in *The Ghosts of Versailles* (Faber 1957), quotes a correspondent from Nairobi who was once a pupil of Miss Jourdain, as saying that on one occasion 'she [Miss Jourdain] unbent sufficiently to tell us, in reply to a question, that she had had several strange psychic visions of Oxford's past rather after the manner of the Versailles experience. She said that she had seen a procession of medieval people, dressed in the attire of the fourteenth or fifteenth century, proceeding down St Margaret's road [which fronts St Hugh's College] to the gallows, the victim on a cart, and the procession singing and dancing and making holiday. She also told us, rather guardedly, that she had had glimpses into the past when walking in the gardens of the college, part of which was once a nunnery. . . .'

Miss Jourdain's evidence in her account of the experiences in the gardens of the Petit Trianon at Versailles has been questioned on the grounds that she was given to 'seeing things' and therefore need not be taken seriously. When we consider that she apparently shared this gift of seeing into the past with Russell, Jung and others who could be quoted, we may, I suggest, be led to pay more attention to what she said she saw (not that it was evidential) than we might otherwise do.

We will end this chapter with Russell's views on the significance of his visions:

Continually in my analysis of the figures I see I am forced to follow them beyond the transitory life I know and to speculate upon the being of the Ever Living. I think there is no half-way house between the spiritual and the material where the intellect can dwell; and if we find we have our being in a universal life we must alter our values, change all our ideas until they depend upon and are in harmony with that sole cause of all that is.

10

The Walkers by the Tower

C. G. JUNG

[On a still night in the late winter or early spring of 1924, when he was alone in Bollingen, the site of the tower which he had built on the upper lake of Zürich, C. G. Jung, the great Swiss psychologist, awoke to the sound of soft footsteps going round the tower. The following excerpt is taken from *Memories, Dreams, Reflections* (Collins and Routledge and Kegan Paul 1963).]

Distant music sounded, coming closer and closer, and then I heard voices laughing and talking. I thought, 'Who can be prowling around? What is this all about? There is only one little footpath along the lake, and scarcely anybody ever walks on it!' While I was thinking these things I became wide awake, and went to the window. I opened the shutters – all was still. There was no one in sight, nothing to be heard – no wind – nothing – nothing at all.

'This is really strange,' I thought. I was certain that the footsteps, the laughter and talk, had been real. But apparently I had only been dreaming. I returned to bed and mulled over the way we can deceive ourselves after all, and what might have been the cause of such a strange dream. In the midst of this, I fell asleep again – and at once the same dream began: once more I heard footsteps, talk, laughter, music. At the same time I had a visual image of several hundred dark-clad figures, possibly peasant boys in their Sunday clothes, who had come down the mountains and were pouring in around the Tower, on

both sides, with a great deal of loud trampling, laughing, singing, and playing of accordions. Irritably, I thought, 'This is
really the limit! I thought it was a dream and now it turns out to
be reality!' At this point, I woke up. Once again I jumped
up, opened the window and shutters, and found everything just
the same as before: a deathly still moonlit night. Then I thought:
'Why, this is simply a case of haunting!'

Naturally I asked myself what it meant when a dream was
so insistent on its reality and at the same time on my being
awake. Usually we experience that only when we see a ghost.
Being awake means perceiving reality. The dream therefore
represented a situation equivalent to reality, in which it created
a kind of wakened state. In this sort of dream, as opposed to
ordinary dreams, the unconscious seems bent on conveying a
powerful impression of reality to the dreamer, an impression
which is emphasized by repetition. The sources of such realities
are known to be physical sensations on the one hand, and archetypal figures on the other.

That night everything was so completely real, or at least
seemed to be so, that I could scarcely sort out the two realities.
Nor could I make anything of the dream itself. What was the
meaning of these music-making peasant boys passing by in a
long procession? It seemed to me they had come out of curiosity, in order to look at the Tower. Never again did I experience
or dream anything similar, and I cannot recall ever having heard
of a parallel to it. . . .

It may be suggested that this is a phenomenon of solitude,
the outward emptiness and silence being compensated by the
image of a crowd of people. This would put it in the same class
with the hallucinations of hermits, which are likewise compen-
satory. But do we know what realities such stories may be
founded on? It is also possible that I had been so sensitized
by the solitude that I was able to perceive the procession of
'departed folk' who passed by.

The explanation of this experience as a psychic compensation never entirely satisfied me, and to say that it was a hallucination seemed to me to beg the question. . . . It would seem most likely to have been a synchronistic phenomenon. Such phenomena demonstrate that premonitions or visions very often have some correspondence in external reality. There actually existed, as I discovered, a real parallel to my experience. In the Middle Ages just such gatherings of young men took place. These were the *Reislaüfer* (mercenaries) who usually assembled in spring, marched from Central Switzerland to Locarno, met at the Casa di Ferro in Minusio and then marched on together to Milan. In Italy they served as soldiers, fighting for foreign princes. My visions, therefore, might have been one of these gatherings which took place regularly each spring when the young men, with singing and jollity, bade farewell to their native land.

I have not included accounts of dreams in this book, and hesitated to a certain extent whether I should include Jung's experience at the Tower, but decided to do so as it seemed to be something more than a dream. As Jung said, 'Never again did I experience or dream anything similar.'

Jung certainly experienced visions when he was awake. The following is an account of one :

Towards the autumn of 1913 the pressure which I had felt was in *me* seemed to be moving outwards, as though there was something in the air. The atmosphere actually seemed to me darker than it had been. It was as though the sense of oppression no longer sprang exclusively from a psychic situation, but from concrete reality. This feeling grew more and more intense.

In October, while I was alone on a journey, I was suddenly seized by an overpowering vision : I saw a monstrous flood covering all the northern and low-lying lands between the North Sea and the Alps. When it came to Switzerland I saw that the mountains grew higher and higher to protect our country. I realized that a frightful catastrophe was in progress. I saw the mightly yellow waves, the floating rubble of civilization, and the drowned bodies of uncounted thousands. Then the whole sea turned to blood. This vision lasted about one hour. I was perplexed and nauseated and ashamed of my weakness.

Two weeks passed; then the vision recurred, under the same conditions, even more vividly than before, and the blood was more emphasized. An inner voice spoke: 'Look at it well; it is wholly real and it will be so. You cannot doubt it.' That winter someone asked me what I thought were the political prospects of the world in the near future. I replied that I had no thoughts on the matter, but that I saw rivers of blood.

I asked myself whether these visions pointed to a revolution, but could not really imagine anything of the sort. And so I drew the conclusion that they had to do with me myself, and decided that I was menaced by a psychosis. The idea of war did not occur to me at all.

One of Jung's strangest experiences occurred in Ravenna at the tomb of the Empress Galla Placidia, who died in A D 450. He says, 'It can scarcely be explained.' During a stormy crossing from Byzantium to Ravenna in the worst of winter the Empress made a vow that if she came through safely she would build a church and have the perils of the sea represented in it. She kept the vow by building the basilica of San Giovanni in Ravenna and having it adorned with mosaics. According to Jung, in the early Middle Ages, San Giovanni, together with its mosaics was destroyed by fire, but in the Ambrosiana in Milan is still to be found a sketch representing Galla Placidia in a boat.

Even on the occasion of my first visit to Ravenna in 1913, the tomb of Galla Placidia seemed to be significant and unusually fascinating. The second time, twenty years later, I had the same feeling. Once more I fell into a strange mood in the tomb of

Galla Placidia; once more I was deeply stirred. I was there with an acquaintance, and we went directly from the tomb into the Baptistery of the Orthodox.

Here, what struck me first was the mild blue light that filled the room; yet I did not wonder about this at all. I did not try to account for its source, and so the wonder of this light without any visible source did not trouble me. I was somewhat amazed because, in place of the windows I remembered having seen on my first visit, there were now four great mosaic frescoes of incredible beauty which, it seemed, I had entirely forgotten. I was vexed to find my memory so unreliable. The mosaic on the south side represented the baptism in the Jordan; the second picture, on the north side, was of the passage of the Children of Israel through the Red Sea; the third, on the east, soon faded from my memory. It might have shown Naaman being cleansed of leprosy in the Jordan; there was a picture on this theme in the old Merian Bible in my library, which was much like the mosaic. The fourth mosaic on the west side of the baptistery, was the most impressive of all. We looked at this one last. It represented Christ holding his hand to Peter, who was sinking beneath the waves. We stood in front of this mosaic for at least twenty minutes and discussed the original ritual of baptism, especially the curious archaic conception of it as an initiation connected with real peril of death. Such initiations were often connected with the peril of death and so served to express the archetypal idea of death and rebirth. Baptism had originally been a real submersion which at least suggested the danger of drowning. I retained the most distinct memory of the mosaic of Peter sinking, and to this day can see every detail before my eyes; the blue of the sea, individual chips of the mosaic, the inscribed scrolls proceeding from the mouths of Peter and Christ, which I attempted to decipher. After we left the baptistery, I went promptly to Alinari to buy photographs of the mosaics, but could not find any. Time was pressing – this was

only a short visit – and so I postponed the purchase until later.
I thought I might order the pictures from Zürich.

When I was back home, I asked an acquaintance who was
going to Ravenna to obtain the pictures for me. He could not
locate them, for he discovered that the mosaics I had described
did not exist. . . . The lady who had been there with me long
refused to believe that 'what she had seen with her own eyes'
had not existed.

Professor Sir Cyril Burt, who reviewed *Memories, Dreams, Reflections* in the December 1963 *Journal* of the SPR, says he
finds Jung's surprise at the curious incident at Ravenna 'a
little hard to understand.' Sir Cyril points out that the Baptistery
of the Orthodox contains some of the finest and most ancient
mosaics in Ravenna. Over the upper arcades of the walls,
amidst golden foliage, there are figures of apostles or prophets
standing out against an intense *blue* background. In the cupola
there is Christ's baptism, the river Jordan with an obscure
figure (usually interpreted as the river god), and the figures of
the disciples, once again with a background of vivid blue.
Certainly there is nothing that resembles the Passage of the
Red Sea or the Rescue of Peter; but these are common subjects
in later baptisteries. Jung himself adds that one of the scenes
which he believed he saw reminded him of 'a picture in the
old Merian Bible in his library'. (Merian's illustrated Bible,
printed in about 1625, also has a picture of the drowning of
Pharaoh's Host and of Christ and Peter.) Moreover, says Sir
Cyril, each of the early baptisteries in Ravenna, like nearly all
the early baptisteries in the Byzantine style, are octagonal; few,
if any, separate baptisteries are square. Jung continually reminds
us that he enjoyed an exceptionally clear visual imagination. Is
it not possible therefore (Sir Cyril asks) that Jung's recollection
of this particular building has become fused with memories of
biblical pictures and of other baptisteries and chapels which he

visited while in Italy, and that the work of the unconscious consisted, not in creating a vision of mosaics that did not exist, but in modifying in memory the details of the mosaics he had actually seen there – doubtless as a result of the common process which Bartlett has termed 'elaboration during recall'?

However, this view hardly takes into account the experience which Jung's companion apparently shared with him. It would be most interesting to have her own account of the visit to Ravenna.

11

The Dream House

AUGUSTUS HARE

[The following story was told to Augustus Hare by a Miss Broke at a house party in Suffolk in November 1894.] A few years ago there was a lady living in Ireland – a Mrs Butler – clever, handsome, popular, prosperous and perfectly happy. One morning she said to her husband, and to anyone who was staying there, 'Last night I had the most wonderful night. I seemed to be spending hours in the most delightful place, in the most enchanting house I ever saw – not large, you know, but just the sort of house one might live in one's self, and oh! so perfectly, so deliciously comfortable. Then there was the loveliest conservatory, and the garden was so enchanting! I wonder if anything half so perfect can really exist.'

And the next morning she said, 'Well, I have been to my house again. I must have been there for hours. I sat in the library: I walked on the terrace; I examined all the bedrooms: and it is simply the most perfect house in the world.' So it grew to be quite a joke in the family. People would ask Mrs Butler in the morning if she had been to her house in the night, and often she had, and always with more intense enjoyment. She would say, 'I count the hours till bedtime, that I may get back to my house!' Then gradually the current of outside life flowed in, and gave a turn to their thoughts: the house ceased to be talked about.

Two years ago the Butlers grew very weary of their life in Ireland. The district was wild and disturbed. The people were insolent and ungrateful. At last they said, 'We are well off, we have no children, there's no reason why we should put up with this, and we'll go and live altogether in England.'

So they came to London, and sent for all the house agents' lists of places within forty miles of London, and many were the places they went to see. At last they heard of a house in Hampshire. They went to it by rail, and drove from the station. As they came to the lodge, Mrs Butler said, 'Do you know, this is the lodge of my house.' They drove down an avenue – 'But this *is* my house!' she said.

When the housekeeper came, she said, 'You will think it very odd, but do you mind my showing *you* the house: that passage leads to the library, and through that there is a conservatory, and then through a window you enter the drawing-room,' etc., and it was all so. At last, in an upstairs passage, they came upon a baize door. Mrs Butler for the first time, looked puzzled. 'But that door is not in my house,' she said. 'I don't understand about your house, ma'am,' said the housekeeper, 'but that door has only been there six weeks.'

Well, the house was for sale, and the price asked was very small, and they decided at once to buy it. But when it was bought and paid for, the price had been so extraordinarily small, that they could not help a misgiving that there must be something wrong with the place. So they went to the agent of the people who had sold it and said, 'Well, now the purchase is made and the deeds are signed, *will* you mind telling us why the price asked was so small?'

The agent had started violently when they came in, but recovered himself. Then he said to Mrs Butler, 'Yes, it is quite true the matter is quite settled, so there can be no harm in telling now. The fact is that the house has had a great reputation for being haunted; but you, madam, need be under no apprehensions, for you are yourself the ghost!'

On the nights when Mrs Butler had dreamt she was at her house, she – her 'astral body' – had been seen there.

This account is taken from the last of the six volumes of *The Story of my Life* by Augustus Hare (George Allen 1900). The author, who died unmarried at the age of sixty-eight in 1903, is described in *The Dictionary of National Biography* as 'a devotée of fashionable culture, and when in England much of his time was spent in visiting country houses, where he was well known as a raconteur of ghost stories'. We do not know who this Mrs Butler was or the address of the house in Hampshire which she was said to haunt. Possibly it was a tale which had grown in the telling by the time it was related to Augustus Hare.

12

The Bottle-Breaking Case

CESARE LOMBROSO

[A criticism often implied in cases in which poltergeist-type phenomena occur is that nothing ever happens when trained and critical investigators are present. Among the admittedly few exceptions is an investigation carried out by Professor Cesare Lombroso, the famous psychiatrist and criminologist, in an Italian inn. Here is his account in *After Death – What?* published by Unwin in London in 1908.]

On the 16th November [1900], in Turin, Via Bava, No. 6, in a little inn kept by a man named Fumero, there began to be heard in the day time, but to a greater extent at night, a series of strange noises. In seeking out the cause, it was found that full or empty wine bottles had been broken in the wine cellar. More frequently they would descend from their places and roll along the floor, heaping themselves against the closed door in such a way as to obstruct the entrance when it was opened. In the sleeping chamber on the upper floor (which communicated by a staircase with the servants' room near the small public room of the inn) garments were twisted up, and some of them transported themselves downstairs into the room beneath. Two chairs in coming down were broken. Copper utensils which had been hung upon the walls of the servants' dining room fell to the floor and slid over long reaches of the room, sometimes getting broken. A spectator put his hat on the bed of the upper chamber; it disappeared and was later found in the filth-heap of the courtyard below.

Careful examination failed to disclose any normal cause for these performances. No help could be got from either the police or the priest. Nay, when the latter was performing his office, a huge bottle full of wine was broken at his very feet. A vase of flowers that had been brought into the inn descended safely on to a table from the moulding above the door, where it had been placed. Two large bottles of rosolio, which they were distilling, were broken in broad daylight. Five or six times, even in the presence of the police, a little staircase ladder, which leaned against the wall at one side of the main room of the inn, was slowly lowered to the floor, yet without hurting anyone. A gun went across the room and was found on the floor in the opposite corner. Two bottles came down from a high shelf with some force. They were not broken, but they bruised the elbow of a porter, giving him a slight 'black-and-blue spot'.

The people kept crowding in to see, and the police during their investigations gave the Fumero family to understand that they suspected them of simulating, so that the poor creatures decided to suffer the annoyance in silence. They even gave out that it had ceased (after an imaginary visit from me), so as to escape at least the guying, if not the damage. I began attentively to study the case.

I made a minute examination of the premises. The rooms were small. Two of them served the purpose of a wine shop; one was used for a servants' eating room, and was connected by a small stairway with a bed-chamber above. Lastly, there was a deep wine cellar, access to which was obtained by means of a long stairway and a passageway. The people informed me that they noticed that whenever anyone entered the cellar the bottles began to be broken. I entered at first in the dark, and, sure enough, I heard the breaking of glasses and the rolling of bottles under my feet. I thereupon lit up the place. The bottles were massed together upon five shelves, one over the other. In the middle of the room was a rude table. I had six lighted candles placed upon this, on the supposition that the spiritualistic phenomena would cease in bright light. On the contrary, I saw three empty bottles, which stood upright on the floor, spin along as if twirled by a finger and break to pieces near my table. To avoid a possible trick I carefully examined by the light of a large candle, and touched with my hand all the full bottles standing on the shelves and ascertained that there were no wires or strings that might explain the movements. After a few minutes two bottles, then four, and later others on the second and third shelves separated themselves from the rest and fell to the floor without any violent motion, but rather as if they had been lifted down by someone; and after this descent, rather than fall, six burst upon the wet floor (already drenched with wine) and two remained intact. A quarter of an hour afterwards three others from the last compartment fell and were broken on the floor. Then I turned to leave the cellar. As I was on the point of going out, I heard the breaking of another bottle on the floor. When the door was shut, all again became quiet.

I came back on another day. They told me that the same phenomena occurred with decreasing frequency, adding that a little brass colour-grinder had sprung from one place to another in the servants' room, and, striking against the opposite wall, jammed itself out of shape – as indeed I observed. Two or three chairs had bounced around with such violence that they were broken, without, however, hurting any one standing by. A table was also broken.

I asked to see and examine all the people of the house. There was a tall waiter lad of thirteen, apparently normal; another, a head-waiter, also normal. The master of the house was a brave old soldier who from time to time threatened the spirits with his gun. Judging from his flushed face and forced hilarity, I judged him to be somewhat under the influence of alcohol. The mistress of the inn was a little woman of some fifty years, lean and very slender. From infancy up she had been subject to tremors, neuralgia, and nocturnal hallucinations, and had had an operation for hystero-ovariotomy. For all these reasons I counselled the husband to have her leave the premises for three days. She went to Nole, her native town, on the 25th November, and there suffered from hallucinations – voices heard at night, movements, persons that no one else saw or heard. But she did not cause any annoying movements of objects. During these days nothing happened at the inn. But as soon as she got back the performances began again, at first furiously, but afterwards more mildly. The occurrences were always the same – utensils, chairs, bottles, broken or displaced. Seeing this, I again counselled that the wife absent herself anew, and she did so on 29 November. On the day the woman left (she was in a state of great excitement and had cursed the alleged spirits), all the dishes and bottles that had been placed on the table were broken and fell to the floor. If the family were going to dine, the table had to be prepared in another place and by another woman, because no dish touched by the mistress remained intact. Hence one naturally suspected that she had mediumistic powers, or would have done so if it had not been that during her absence *the phenomena were repeated in just the same way*. That is to say (to be specific), a pair of shoes of hers that were in the bed-chamber, on the dressing-cloth, came downstairs in broad daylight (half-past eight in the morning), traversed the servants' room through the air, passed into the common room of the inn and there fell down at the feet of two customers who were seated at a table. (This was on 27 November.) The shoes were replaced on the dressing-cloth and continually watched, but did not move again until noon of the next day; and at that hour, when all were at dinner, they disappeared entirely! A week afterwards they were found, with heels to the floor, under the bed of the same chamber.

Another pair of ladies' shoes, placed in the same chamber, on the dressing-cloth, and carefully watched, disappeared, and were found only after the lapse of twenty days (folded up as if they were to be packed in a trunk), between the mattresses of a bed in the same chamber that had been turned upside down in vain *two days after the disappearance*.

When it was seen that the phenomena continued just the same, the woman was recalled from Nole, and they were repeated with the same continuity as before. A bottle of effervescent liquor, for example, in the inn, in full daylight, in the sight of everybody, slowly, as if accompanied by a human hand, passed over a distance of twelve or fifteen feet, as far as the servants' room, the door of which was open, and then fell to the floor and was broken.

After all this it occurred to the host to dismiss the younger of his two waiters. When he left (7 December) all the phenomena ceased. This of course makes one surmise that the motive force emanated from him. Yet he was not an hysteric, and was the cause of no spiritistic occurrences in his new home.

Now for a word about Professor Lombroso, who was born on 18 November 1836 and died in 1909. His first important appointment was as Professor of Psychiatry at Pavia in 1869. Later he became director of a lunatic asylum at Pesaro. At the time of the investigation given above he was Professor of Forensic Medicine and Psychiatry at Turin. His theory that when suspects tell lies under interrogation their blood pressure suddenly changes led him to invent the first 'lie detector'. This theory has had the support of later criminologists, but another of Professor Lombroso's contentions, that criminals belong to a specialized anthropological type marked by physical and psychological characteristics, now has little support.

Until Professor Lombroso was forty-six he regarded all spiritualistic manifestations with utter contempt. He changed his mind about this as the result of two sittings he had with Eusapia

Palladino, the famous Neopolitan medium, in 1890. Indeed it was Lombroso who brought her to the attention of the learned world.

It is interesting to note the movement of the bottles described by Professor Lombroso as 'without any violent motion, but rather as if they had been lifted down by someone'. In his book *Ghosts and Poltergeists* (Burns and Oates 1963) Father Herbert Thurston points out: 'When telekinetic phenomena occur – and this is almost invariably the case – whether they take the form of missiles which seem to come from nowhere, or of crockery, and even furniture crashing or flying through the air, the movement often seems to be controlled, tortuous and at variance with the laws of gravitation.' He quotes in support of this view a statement by Professor W. F. Barrett, FRS, in volume fifteen of *Proceedings* of the SPR: 'The movement of objects is usually quite unlike that due to gravitational and other attraction. They slide about, rise in the air, move in eccentric paths, sometimes in a leisurely manner, often turn round in their career, and usually descend quietly without hurting the observers.'

The disturbances stopped when a waiter aged thirteen was dismissed. Barrett has pointed out that the manifestations in poltergeist-type outbreaks seem to depend upon the presence of some particular individual – usually a young person and often a child – who must be assumed to possess strange, if unconscious, mediumistic powers. It will have been noted that Lombroso was presumably alone in the cellar when the bottles broke in his presence. This remains a very puzzling case.

13

The Sauchie Poltergeist

A. R. G. OWEN

About mid-December 1960 I learned of the Sauchie (Scotland) case from press cuttings kindly lent me by Mr Trevor H. Hall, J.P. It appeared that abundant, supposed poltergeist, activity occurred between 22 November and 2 December, being centred on an eleven-year-old child, Virginia Campbell. The newspaper had reported statements by a number of witnesses of standing in the local community, which though guarded were definite. This encouraged me to believe that some of the happenings might have been genuinely paranormal. This impression was somewhat confirmed as the result of enquiries by letter and telephone. It also appeared likely that if I visited the locality at least some of the witnesses would be prepared to supply detailed accounts of their experiences. It seemed best to allow time for the passage of Christmas, New Year's Day and the school holidays. I therefore arranged to stay in Alloa from the evening of Friday 13 January until Monday 16 January. To my great good fortune I was able to interview no fewer than five responsible persons who had each witnessed some unusual phenomena and observed it critically, namely:

– The Rev. T. W. Lund (MA, BD), Minister of Sauchie (Church of Scotland), resident at Manse of Sauchie, Sauchie Main Street;

– Dr W. H. Nisbet (MB, ChB), physician, resident at Hilden, Stirling Street, Tillicoultry;

– Dr William Logan (MB, ChB), physician, resident at Beechwood, Dollar Road, Tillicoultry, in practice with Dr Nisbet;

– Mrs Sheila Logan (MB, ChB, DPH), Dr Logan's wife, and herself a qualified physician;

– Miss Margaret Stewart, resident at 61 Jamieson Gardens, Tillicoultry, a fully qualified teacher on the staff of Sauchie Primary School.

Decisive importance attached to the testimony of these witnesses for reasons that will indeed be obvious. By nature of their vocations they may be expected to have well trained and disciplined minds, and their probity may be taken as axiomatic. Again, they are independent witnesses, free of family ties with the disturbed household. . . .

The background to the case is as follows. Virginia Campbell is eleven years old and the youngest child of elderly parents, Mr James Campbell and Mrs Annie Campbell (aged fifty-six). They are citizens of Eire, all their children having been born there. Virginia's life was spent in County Donegal, her father having worked a farm or croft at or near Moville. Her upbringing was extremely quiet and lonely, the other children having all grown up and left home. Most of them appear at various times to have come over to settle in England or Scotland. The only regular companions that Virginia had at Moville other than her parents were her pet dog Toby and one friend, a little girl, Anna. . . .

In mid-October 1960 Virginia started to attend Sauchie Primary School. Mr Hill, the headmaster, records that when Mrs Campbell brought her to school for enrolment they both created a curious impression on him. Mrs Campbell 'offered no more information other than was necessary and her voice seemed to come unwillingly from behind the mask of her face'. Again, 'they gave the impression of people who had lived for a long time in a remote and isolated place, whose reality was a blend of their immediate environment and the boundless vision of the mind'. . . . At first she [Virginia] was extremely shy, and her teacher, Miss Margaret Stewart, found it difficult to establish real communication with her. This ascribed not only to her shyness but also to the language difficulty, there being a difference in speech between Donegal and Clackmannanshire. Apart from this, Miss Stewart found her a completely normal little girl. In the course of time Miss Stewart was able to form a more detailed picture of Virginia's personality. It is an attractive one. Undoubtedly she missed her father very much. However, despite her shyness, she makes durable friendships easily. She is somewhat above normal intelligence. A test estimated her IQ at 111, but for obvious reasons the figure is probably too low. She is becoming interested in and more proficient at academic subjects. By March 1961 much of her shyness had worn off and she was very much more forthcoming. Virginia is very creative with her hands. She has a typical girl's interests, is uninhibited in physical activities and is fond of dancing. Outwardly she is always placid and unemotional. She is obedient, has a mature outlook and discharges responsible tasks well. She is on good terms with her classmates.

Virginia is a big girl for her age. With the rest of the family at Park Crescent [Virginia was staying there with her brother and sister-in-law and their two children, Virginia's niece and nephew, Margaret, age nine and Derek, age six] she had been under Dr Nisbet's medical care. Her health is good, as she has needed no treatment except a routine polio injection. There is no sign of any fundamental psychological abnormality. Thus, generally speaking, her physical and mental health are basically sound. However, it may be of significance that at present she is going through a period of extremely rapid physical development and maturation (Dr Owen's report was written in the spring of 1961). Puberty in the full sense has not arrived but she is going through a very rapid pubescence. It may also be of significance that on occasions during the poltergeist disturbances she did give some indication of mental or emotional turmoil. At times she talked in her sleep, showing signs of both upset and aggressiveness. But when account is taken of all the factors, this cannot in itself be taken as evidence of basic mental ill health.

I visited the Campbell house at 19 Park Crescent. It is a very comfortable, well appointed and well kept home. Mr and Mrs Thomas Campbell, who bear an excellent local reputation, seemed to me to be very respectable, sensible and intelligent people. The three children came back from Sunday School while I was there. As far as I could see the family relationships between all five seemed normal and happy. By this time (mid-January 1961) Virginia seemed to have accommodated herself to the existence of the poltergeist, and even to have pride and interest in it or 'him', because she had christened him 'Wee Hughie'.

I have selected from the witnesses' statements those events which convinced them as being paranormal. In some cases I have indicated in brief their reasons for so concluding. The statements themselves . . . go into the question of proof much more amply, as well as providing a great deal of subsidiary information that may well be relevant both to interpretation of this case and the evaluation of poltergeist cases generally. I have also included an account of Virginia's 'trances'.

Tuesday, 22 November When Virginia and Margaret went to bed a 'thunking' noise, like a bouncing ball, was heard in the bedroom, and then on the stairs and in the living-room when they came down. As with all subsequent manifestations it ceased entirely when Virginia went to sleep.

Wednesday, 23 November Virginia was kept home from school. At teatime Mr and Mrs Thomas Campbell were in the living-room. Virginia was sitting in an armchair next to a sideboard. They saw the sideboard move out five inches from the wall and then move back again. Virginia was not touching it.

That evening when Virginia was in bed but not asleep loud knocks, audible all over the house, were heard by the family and several neighbours and by the Rev. Mr Lund, who was called in about midnight. He found the knocking to come from the bed head in circumstances that proved it was not being struck or shaken by Virginia or by anyone else. Mr Lund gripped the bed head and felt it vibrating during the knocking. Mr Lund saw a large linen chest (twenty-seven inches long, seventeen inches high and fourteen inches wide, and full of bed linen) rock and raise itself slightly, travel a distance of eighteen inches over the linoleum and then move back.

When at length it was suggested that Margaret go back into the double bed with Virginia there was a burst of violent and peremptory knocking.

Thursday, 24 November Virginia stayed at home again from school. In the evening Mr Lund saw Virginia's pillow rotated from its normal position horizontally through 60 degrees. Her head was on the pillow but it seemed quite impossible that she could do this herself. He also heard some knocking and saw rockings of the linen chest.

Dr. Nisbet heard knockings and a sawing noise. He saw a peculiar rippling or puckering motion pass over the surface of the pillow. Virginia's head was on the pillow but he saw no way in which she could produce this effect.

Friday, 25 November Virginia stayed home again in the morning but was taken to school in the afternoon. During a period of silent reading, Miss Stewart saw Virginia trying to hold down the lid of her desk, which raised itself steeply on its hinge two or three times. Miss Stewart was able to see that Virginia was not raising it herself by movement of her limbs.

A little later on the desk behind Virginia, which was temporarily unoccupied, was seen by Miss Stewart to rise slowly about an inch off the floor. It then settled down gently a little out of its original position. Miss Stewart went straight over to it and verified that no strings, levers, or anything else had been in operation.

In the evening Dr Nisbet kept watch in Virginia's bedroom before she went to sleep. He heard spells of knocking, even when Virginia was lying motionless on the bed without bedclothes. From time to time he saw the linen chest, which was standing in isolation, move distances of about a foot. Once the lid opened and shut several times in succession.

He observed horizontal rotations of the pillow through as much as ninety degrees. As with the pillow on the Thursday, a curious ripple would pass over the bedclothes from time to time. It could be described as a 'puckering', as if due to traction by an invisible agency.

Saturday, 26 November Dr Logan sat in the bedroom. He saw a slight puckering of the coverlet and a rotary motion of the pillow towards Virginia's body.

Sunday, 27 November In the morning Dr Logan took his dog to 19 Park Crescent. Virginia was much taken with him and said he reminded her of her dog Toby.

No paranormal phenomena are reported for that evening. But there was one event of great interest. When Virginia went to bed she went into a 'trance'. She talked in her sleep, calling for her friend Anna and for Toby, both left behind in Ireland. At 11.30 Mr Lund called. Virginia was then up but went back to bed and fell asleep but called for Toby. She was given a teddy bear. She flung it away, crying out vehemently and striking out violently with her hands. They decided to leave the room and she fell into a normal sleep.

Monday, 28 November Virginia went to school in the morning. About 10.15 the class was working a problem paper. Virginia came up to Miss Stewart's desk (a table four feet long by two feet wide) for help. She stood to the left of Miss Stewart's chair and somewhat away from the table with her hands clasped behind her back. While Miss Stewart was sketching out the solution to the problem, a blackboard pointer lying on top of the desk started to vibrate and moved on top of the desk until it reached the edge and fell off. Miss Stewart put her hand on the desk and felt it vibrating. The desk was moving. The right-hand end travelled away so that the desk swung round. In the afternoon Virginia was taken to stay with a relative at Dollar. Dr Nisbet visited her there in the evening. Loud knockings were audible all over the house.

Tuesday, 29 November Dr Logan and his wife, Dr Sheila Logan, visited Virginia at Dollar in the evening. They heard several outbreaks of knocking. These varied from gentle tappings to violent agitated raps, these later occurring when they were about to leave. The sound appeared to come from the vicinity of Virginia. Mrs Logan had previously been sceptical about the reported manifestations but satisfied herself that the noises came from within the room, but were not caused by the activity of anyone in it.

As soon as they got home to Tillicoultry Dr Logan was summoned by telephone back to Dollar, as Virginia was now in another 'trance'. He found her talking in a loud and unnatural voice, calling for Toby and Anna, and throwing herself about the bed. Her eyes were closed but she heard and answered questions. Her replies indicated a lack of normal inhibition as if repressed thoughts were emerging. She awoke after ten minutes in a normal state of mind and asked for a cup of tea.

Wednesday, 30 November Virginia returned to Sauchie. The family reported that there were no phenomena that night.

Thursday, 1 December Dr Nisbet and Dr Logan set up a movie camera in Virginia's bedroom, as well as arrangements for sound recording, before she came up to bed at 9 p.m. From then until 10.30 there were continual noises (ranging from barely perceptible tappings to agitated knocks) and occasional rippling of the bedclothes. Between 10.30 and 11 a considerable amount of hysterical talking by Virginia was recorded, in which she showed

84

the same lack of inhibition as she had previously in her 'trances'.

At 11 p.m. the Rev. Mr Lund and three other ministers arrived to conduct a service of intercession (*not* of exorcism). During the service (11.15 to 11.30) there were some knockings.

A variety of noises were recorded between 11.30 and 12.15. Three examples were later recorded by the BBC and used in a regional sound broadcast feature called 'Scope', which gave a brief review of the case. These noises were: (*a*) a series of loud peremptory knocks; (*b*) a harsh, rasping, sawing noise; and (*c*) a scream from Virginia when the lid of the linen box went up. (When I visited him on 13 January 1961, Dr Logan kindly replayed for me a recording of the whole item from the broadcast. Both the knocks and the sawing were very loud and harsh.)

Subsequent to 1 December, the phenomena appear to have been less pronounced and troublesome. The Rev. Mr Lund and the doctor thought it best that publicity should die out and therefore, very reasonably, announced that a 'cure' had been effected, or at least nearly so. It would seem that genuine phenomena either ceased or occurred with diminished frequency and violence. In any case little that is evidential has been reported since 1 December. . . . One occurrence I do regard as well attested because it is reported by Miss Stewart. Also, it may be significant because it took place about two lunar months after the very disturbed Friday, 25 November.

Monday, 23 January 1961 Virginia placed a bowl of bulbs on Miss Stewart's desk in the classroom. It moved across the top of the desk in a manner similar to the pointer on 28 November, fifty-six days before.

This extract is taken from *Can We Explain the Poltergeist?* by A. R. G. Owen (Helix Press, New York 1964). Dr Owen, a Fellow of Trinity College, Cambridge, is director of the New

Dr. Owen has also written *Science and the Spook* which was published by Garrett Publications.

Horizons Research Foundation, Toronto, Canada. He is a geneticist.

Dr Owen gives a list of less well-attested events. Among these is a report by Virginia's father that, while he was staying in the house, an apple floated out of a fruit bowl, and also that his shaving brush had flown round the bathroom.

Dr Owen says: ' It will be seen from the diary of the main events that the five witnesses believe themselves to have heard certain sounds and seen certain movements of objects. It is just possible in principle to suppose that one person could be the victim of illusion or hallucination. It is, however, beyond all possibility that five responsible persons should be so deceived at various occasions over a period of two weeks. Thus we must conclude that they heard actual noises and saw actual motions of real objects.'

The reality of the observations being established, says Dr Owen, we need, of course, to consider possible normal explanations, i.e. in terms of known physical or human agencies. Since trickery had been found applicable in some well-known cases, some writers had shown a tendency to explain all cases of poltergeist-haunted children by a 'naughty little girl' theory. As the Campbell household comprised three children, it was worth noting that the Rev. Mr Lund, the three physicians and Miss Stewart all took account of the possibility of trickery and excluded it on the basis of the evidence. Miss Stewart carefully noted whether it was possible for Virginia to have moved either Miss Stewart's desk or her own desk lid, and immediately searched for any mechanism by which the desk behind Virginia could have been levitated. Dr Nisbet and Dr Logan were both convinced that the rippling or puckering of the bedcovers was not consistent with elevation from below by Virginia's hands. Dr Nisbet's observations of the puckering of the surface of the pillow seems inexplicable as the result of action by Virginia. Movements of the whole pillow seen by Mr Lund, Dr Nisbet and Dr Logan on various occasions cannot credibly be supposed to derive from movements of Virginia's head, neck or shoulders.

Again, Mr Lund saw the linen chest move when Virginia's feet were well tucked in – she was supine in the bed, and no one else was near it. Dr Nisbet's observations of the movement of the linen chest and its lid were under similar conditions and equally exclude trickery. Knockings were heard when Virginia was lying on top of the bed without bedclothes and seen to be motionless. In any case, the Rev. Mr Lund, Dr Nisbet and Dr and Mrs Logan all became quite satisfied that the tapping, knocking and sawing noises, often very loud, could not be explained by the shaking of the bed. Dr Logan experimented in the production of sawing noises, he told me, by drawing a fingernail over various surfaces such as bedsheets or carpets. He succeeded in producing a rasping noise but much weaker in intensity and somewhat different in tone and quality from the sawing noise as heard and recorded. All observers agreed that the sounds appeared to originate in the room where Virginia was and were not consistent with their fraudulent production outside the room.

'To sum up,' says Dr Owen, 'it seems evident that the physical phenomena observed by the key witnesses are incompatible with trickery by Virginia, or by other children or adults.'

Dr Owen considers, and rejects, a theory that the noises heard and the displacement of objects could have been caused by earth movements owing to subsidence, underground water or tidal action. 'According to my own observations, Sauchie School and 19 Park Crescent and the surrounding properties show no sign of slipping, foundering or cracking,' he states.

What explanation can be put forward then for these strange happenings?

Dr Owen says:

As regards causation, the happenings seemed to the Rev. Mr Lund as being, on balance, more consistent with the functioning of a force or forces originating in Virginia than with the operation of a discarnate entity. Dr Logan and Miss Stewart, independently of one another and of Mr Lund, both very definitely put forward the same interpretation. On the evidence this finding is much to be preferred to any other. The association between occurrences and the near presence of Virginia is complete ' It ' therefore was fairly closely linked to Virginia's physical presence. There is no evidence of any disembodied entity functioning. Economy of hypothesis thus suggests that as a result of a peculiar condition at the relevant times in Virginia's body or mind certain unknown physical forces operated on matter in the vicinity. This is the best physical conclusion.

I regard this case as a most interesting one, chiefly because a number of people whose training made them unbiased observers were able to investigate the phenomena in good light. All were on the lookout for trickery. As the late Mr W. H. Salter, a leading figure in the SPR for many years, said in his book *Zoar* (Sidgwick and Jackson 1961), ' It is extremely rare for a critical observer, who knows what trickery can effect, to be present when the phenomena are occurring.'

Dr Owen draws comparisons between the Sauchie case and some others in the literature of psychical research. I can add to this list. For instance, in the ' bottle popping ' case in Seaford, Long Island, in 1958, which I dealt with in *The Unexplained,* the disturbances, which seemed to centre round James Herrmann, a twelve-year-old schoolboy, included twenty-three incidents in which screw-top bottles were opened when, apparently, no one in the house had opened them. At Sauchie the bed that Virginia shared with Margaret was twice soaked as a result of a loosening of the stoppers of hot water bottles, even though they were tightly screwed up when put in the bed.

A most unusual feature of the Sauchie case was the ripple that passed over the pillow on which Virginia's head was resting ' as if due to traction by an invisible agency '. It is difficult to ascribe this to any natural cause. After my last book, *Apparitions and*

Ghosts, was published I received a letter from a consultant psychiatrist describing how, when he was staying in a house in the North of England in 1968, he was awakened in the early hours of the morning by what sounded like a hand patting the pillow between his head and the wall. This was done twice. The first time it woke him up and then, while he was wide awake, it was repeated. He added, 'We had dined early and I had had only water to drink.'

When I discussed his experiences with the doctor I found out that he had not read Dr Owen's book.

It is difficult to disagree with Dr Owen when he says, 'In my opinion the Sauchie case must be regarded as establishing beyond all reasonable doubt the objective reality of some poltergeist phenomena.'

14

The Worksop Case

FRANK PODMORE

At the beginning of March 1883 the *Retford and Gainsborough Times* and other local papers gave accounts of some remarkable disturbances that had occurred in the first two or three days of the month at the house of a small horse-dealer in Worksop [Nottinghamshire] named Joe White. One or two members of the Society [the SPR] entered into communication with the principal persons named in the newspaper reports, and with a friend in the neighbourhood, who very kindly took some trouble in inquiring into the matter for the Society. But it soon became obvious that, as nearly all the witnesses of the occurrences related were uneducated and unable, therefore, to write a coherent account of what had happened, the best way to arrive at the truth of the matter was for one of us to go in person to make inquiries. Accordingly, at the request of the Haunted House Committee, I went down to Worksop on the afternoon of Saturday 7 April with the intention of inspecting the actual scene of the occurrences, and of personally interrogating the principal witnesses, in order, if possible, to arrive at some rational explanation of the business. I spent the Saturday evening and the whole of the following day in my inquiries, and have, I think, obtained as intelligible and trustworthy a history of the matter as the lapse of time, the nature of the phenomena themselves and the character of the witnesses will permit.

I derived my information from seven principal eye-witnesses of the disturbances, whom I interrogated, with the single exception of White himself, *separately*. I wrote out the statement of each witness in full immediately after the interview, and the three most important witnesses, Higgs, Currass and White, subsequently read through my notes and signed them. The depositions of these three persons are printed in full below. My time was too short to allow a second interview with the four other principal witnesses, and I was unable, therefore, to obtain their signatures to the depositions; but I have incorporated the statements of all the principal witnesses in my report.

Besides the seven chiefly concerned, I questioned, in the presence of White and his wife, three or four other witnesses of the disturbances: White's brother Tom, a bright-looking lad of eighteen or twenty; Solomon Wass and his wife, next-door neighbours of the Whites, the former an ordinary working-class Northcountryman, the latter a pleasant-looking, intelligent woman; and George ('Buck') Ford, a man of about twenty-eight. From these I obtained general confirmation of the various incidents, as described by White, Higgs and the others, at which they had themselves been present; but time did not permit of much cross-questioning, nor of taking down their evidence in full.

White's house has been built, according to his own statement, about seven years. He has resided in it only three years. I was unable to discover anything about the former occupants. The house stands at the end of a piece of wasteland called the New Building Ground, with another house or cottage attached, the nearest separate building being a public house, about a hundred yards off. With that exception, there are no other buildings within about two hundred yards. There is no entrance to the house by the front, the front door being locked and the joints secured with paper from the inside. Entrance is obtained by a covered passage, open at either end, which separates the two houses, and gives access immediately to a yard, surrounded on one side by high palings and on the other three by piggeries, stables and the two houses. . . . The kitchen is about fifteen feet square. The upper floor is divided into two rooms, the back one, corresponding to the kitchen, being used as a bedroom for Tom and the children; the front one as a store-house for bacon, articles of equipment for horses, and various odds and ends. There is also a garrett above this, into which I did not enter, it being at the time full of bacon in salt. The whole house, not excepting the bedrooms, is hung with bacon, the very staircase being lined with it, so that I had to draw my coat close to me in going up. A large part of the bacon, I was told by White, had gone bad during the period of the disturbances.

The front or inner room on the ground floor was an ordinary room, like all the rest of the house half-filled with bacon, and containing, besides bedroom furniture, a large beer barrel on trestles; everything in it filthily dirty.

I looked all over the house in daylight, but could discern no holes in the walls or ceilings, nor any trace of the extensive and elaborate machinery that would have been required to produce the movements by ordinary mechanical means.

The history of the disturbances, as gathered from the various witnesses whom I interrogated, appears to be briefly as follows.

Nothing remarkable had been seen or heard in the house until about 20 or 21 February 1883 when, as Mrs White was alone with two of the children in the kitchen one evening, washing up the tea things at the table, the table tilted up at a considerable angle; the candle was upset, and the wash tub saved only by Mrs W. holding it. She positively assured me that she exerted no pressure whatever upon the table, and the whole incident struck her as very extraordinary. Her husband made light of it at the time.

On Monday, 26th February White was absent from home until the Wednesday afternoon. On the Monday his wife allowed a girl, Eliza Rose, the child of an imbecile mother, to come into the house and share her bed at night. White returned on Wednesday night, but left on the following morning until Friday afternoon. During that one night the girl slept on the squab. On Thursday night, 1 March, at about 11 p.m. Tom White went up to bed – the children having gone up some hours before. At about 11.30, Mrs White and Eliza Rose being alone in the kitchen, various things, such as a corkscrew, clothes pegs and, a saltcellar which had been in the kitchen only a few minutes before, came tumbling step by step down the kitchen stairs. Tom positively and solemnly denied having thrown the articles, and the mystery was increased when, at least twenty minutes after he had gone upstairs, no one having left the room in the interval, some *hot* coals were thrown down.

On the following night, 2 March, at about the same hour – White, Mrs White and Rose being in the kitchen – a noise was heard as of someone coming down the passage between the two houses and stopping just outside the outer door. White told Rose to open the door, but she was too frightened to do so. Then they heard a surcingle (a girth for a horse or other animal) and immediately afterwards some pieces of carpet (being) thrown down the stairs. Then followed some knives and forks and other things. The girl picked them up; but they followed still faster. White left the room to go up to Tom. During his absence one of the ornaments flew off the mantelpiece into the corner of the room near the door. Nothing was seen by the two women; but they heard it fall and found it there. Their screams summoned White down; as he entered the room his candle went out, and something struck him on the forehead. The girl picked up the candle – which appears to have left the candlestick – and two new ones which had not been in the house previously, from the ground; and as soon as a candle was lit, a little china figure of a woman left the mantelpiece and fell into the corner, where it was seen by White. As soon as it was replaced it flew across the room again, and was broken. Other things followed. The women were very frightened, and White, thinking that the disturbances presaged the death of his child, who was very ill from an abscess in the back, sent Tom (who was afraid to go alone) with Ford to fetch the doctor. Mrs White meanwhile took one of the children next door. Rose approached the inner room to fetch one of the others, when things immediately began to fly about and smash themselves in that room. After this all appear to have been absent from the house for a short time. White then returned with Higgs, a policeman, and, while they were alone in the kitchen, standing near the door, a glass jar flew out of the cupboard into the yard; a tumbler also fell from the chest of drawers in the kitchen, when only Higgs was near it. Both then went into the inner room, and found the chest of drawers there turned up on end and smashed. On their return they found Rose, Wass and Tom White in the kitchen (?and Mrs Wass), and all saw a cream jug, which Rose had just placed on the bin, fly four feet up in the air and smash on the floor. Dr Lloyd and Mrs White then entered, and in the presence of all these witnesses a basin was seen to rise slowly from the bin – no person being near it except Dr Lloyd and Higgs. It touched the ceiling, and then fell suddenly to the floor, and was smashed. This was at 12 p.m. All then left except Tom White and his brother. The disturbances continued until about 2 a.m., when all grew quiet, and the Whites slept. At about 8 a.m. on Saturday the third the disturbances began again.

White left the kitchen to attend to some pigs; and in his absence Mrs White and Rose were left alone in the kitchen. A nearly empty port wine bottle leaped up from the table about four feet in the air and fell into a bucket of milk, standing on the table, from which Mrs White was filling some jugs.

Then Currass appears to have been attracted to the scene. He entered with White, young Wass and others and viewed the inner room. They had just returned to the kitchen, leaving the inner door empty and the door of communication open, when the American clock, which hung over the bed, was heard to strike. (It had not done so for eighteen months.) A crash was then heard, and Currass, who was nearest the door, looked in, and found that the clock had fallen over the bed – about four feet broad – and was lying on the floor.[1] Shortly afterwards – no one being near it – a china dog flew off the mantelpiece and smashed itself in the corner near the door. Currass and some others then left.

Some plates, a cream jug and other things then flew up in the air, and smashed themselves in view of all who were in the kitchen – Rose, the Whites, and Mrs Wass. White then lay down on the sofa; but disturbances continued during his siesta. In particular, some pictures on the wall next to the pantry began to move, but were taken down at once by his brother. At about 2 p.m. a Salvation Army woman came in and talked to White. Rose was alone with them in the kitchen. A candlestick flew from the bin and fell behind the Salvation Army woman as she stood near the pantry door. She left the room in terror.

Other things then followed at intervals. A full medicine bottle fell without breaking. An empty medicine bottle and a lamp-glass fell and broke. It was then about 4 p.m. and White could stand it no longer. He told the girl she must go; she did in fact leave before 5 p.m. After her departure nothing whatever of an abnormal character took place, and the house has remained undisturbed up to the present time.

With regard to the positions of the persons present, in relation to the objects moved, it may be stated generally that there was no possibility in most cases of the objects having been thrown by

[1] It will be noted that there is a discrepancy between White's and Currass's version of this incident. Mrs White, however, confirmed her husband's account; and I have little doubt that the statement in the text is substantially accurate. Currass is more likely than White to have been mistaken in his recollection of White's position at the time; and Currass's account of his own position does not differ greatly from that given by White. The material point, and one on which both witnesses are agreed, is that no one *saw* the clock fall. Currass's written statement is not clear on this point, but he told me viva voce that his attention was drawn to what had taken place by hearing the crash. Only then did he turn round and saw the clock lying on the floor – (FP, April 1883).

hand. It will be seen, on reference to the depositions of the witnesses that are appended, that the objects were frequently moved in a remote corner of the room, or even in an adjoining room. Moreover, the character of the movements, in many cases, was such as to preclude the possibility of the objects having been thrown.

Of course the obvious explanation of these occurrences is trickery on the part of some of the persons present. In regard to this, it seems to me a matter of very little significance that most of the educated people in Worksop believe White himself to have caused the disturbances. For most educated persons, as we know, would not be ready to admit any other than a mechanical explanation; and if such an explanation be adopted, White, the owner of the house, a man of considerable intelligence, whose record was not entirely clean and who was himself present on the occasion of nearly all the disturbances, must obviously be the agent. But while believing White to be at the bottom of the matter, none of the persons with whom I conversed was prepared with any explanation of his *modus operandi*. That he should have thrown the things was universally admitted to be impossible. And beyond this, I could discover little more than an unquestioning faith in the omnipotence of electricity. No one professed to have any idea of what mechanical means could have been employed, or how they could have been adapted to the end in view. Still less did anyone pretend to have discovered any indications in the house itself of any machinery having been used. Moreover, there was a total absence of any apparent motive on White's part, even supposing that he was capable of effecting the movements himself : while he was unquestionably a considerable loser – to the extent of nearly £9 as estimated by himself, though this estimate is probably exaggerated[2] – by the articles broken, he appears to have reaped no corresponding

[2] We must remember that £9 in 1883 represented quite a respectable sum in a working-class household. Today's equivalent would be £66.

advantage. The one motive that I heard suggested – if we disregard a report in one newspaper, subsequently contradicted in another, to the effect that White was anxious to buy the house, and to buy it cheap – was that he produced the disturbances in fulfilment of a sporting bet. But I saw no reason to regard this explanation as anything but a scholium evolved by some ingenious commentator from the facts themselves.

Again, had White himself been the principal agent in the matter, it is clear that he must have had at least two confederates, for he was not himself present during the disturbances on the Thursday night – which might, indeed, have been caused by his brother Tom – nor was either he or his brother present during some of the occurrences on the following day. Moreover, these confederates must not only have been extremely skilful, but they must have been capable of more than ordinary reticence and self control. For it is remarkable that, with the single exception of the statements made by the girl Rose, no one professed to have heard even a hint from White himself, from his brother, or from any other of any trickery in the matter.

Moreover, it is hard to conceive by what mechanical appliances, under the circumstances described, the movements could have been effected. The clock, for instance – a heavy American one – was thrust out from the wall in a horizontal direction, so as apparently to clear a four-foot bedstead that lay immediately beneath it, and the nail from which it depended remained *in situ* on the wall. The objects thrown about in the kitchen moved generally, but by no means always, in the direction of the outer door. And it is noticeable that, in most cases, they do not appear to have been thrown, but in some manner borne or wafted across the room; for, though they fell on a stone floor fifteen or sixteen feet distant, they were often unbroken, and were rarely shivered. And it is impossible to reconcile the account given of the movement of some other objects, variously described as 'jerky', 'twirling', and 'turning over and over', with the supposition that the objects depended on any fixed support, or were in any way suspended.

Lastly, to suppose that these various objects were all moved by mechanical contrivances argues incredible stupidity, amounting almost to imbecility, on the part of all the persons present who were not in the plot. That the movement of the arms necessary to set the machinery in motion should have passed unobserved on each and every occasion by all the witnesses is almost impossible. Not only so, but Currass, Higgs and Dr Lloyd, all independent observers, assured me that they examined some of the objects which had been moved, immediately after the occurrences, with the express intention of discovering, if possible, any clue to an explanation of the matter, but entirely failed to do so. These men were not over-credulous; they certainly were not wanting in intelligence; and they were not, any of them, prepossessed in favour of White. But they each admitted that they could discover no possible explanation of the disturbances, and were fairly bewildered by the whole matter.

Statement of Joe White
(White was a fair witness. I think that he always intended to speak the truth, but that occasionally his memory proved treacherous. In all important points, however, he was corroborated by his wife (an excellent witness), Higgs and Currass – FP.)

I returned home about 7 on the Friday night [2 March]. I had been absent from home on Monday and Tuesday night; and it was during my absence that my wife took in the girl Rose, who shared her bed in the front inner room. I slept at home on Wednesday, and the girl then slept on the squab in the kitchen. I left again on Thursday morning, and returned as mentioned on the Friday.

When told by my wife and Tom what had happened on Thursday night, I said someone must have been tricking, and didn't think much more about it. But I chaffed the lass [Rose] a good deal, for she was much frightened. About 11.30 on Friday evening, when my wife, the girl, and I were alone in the kitchen, just going up to bed, I heard a noise as if someone had come down the passage between the two houses, and were standing just outside our door. They didn't knock; but I said to Rose, ' Go and see who's there.' But she was frightened and didn't go. Then presently a lot of things came rattling down the stairs. I don't know what came first: but a lot of things came – a surcingle, bits of carpet, knives and forks, a corkscrew, etc. The girl went to pick them up, and put them on the table, and just as fast as she put them on more things came down. Then my wife said to me, ' The salt cellar came down last night, but you won't have it down tonight, for here it is on the table '. She was using it at the time for salting Tom's dinner for next day. She had hardly said this, when the salt cellar flew off the table, and into the corner near the outer door. Rose was in that corner, and not near the table: my wife was at the table, but certainly didn't touch the cellar. I saw the thing go, though I couldn't believe my eyes. My wife didn't see it go, but we both saw it as it struck the wall in the corner. All the salt was spilled out of it. I fairly couldn't believe my own eyes; but I couldn't help thinking it must be Tom. So I went upstairs to him and told him to leave off. ' Thou'lt frighten our Liz to death'. He said, ' It's not me, I'll take my oath it isn't. I've never thrown nowt down.' While I was still talking to him, I heard a crash downstairs; and the women screamed; and my wife cried, ' Come down, Joe '. As I was just coming into the room the candle which I held in my hand went out – I don't know how at all – and we were left in darkness, except for the firelight. Then something hit me on the forehead, and I cried out, ' Who threw that?' Then there was a crash in the corner. I found out when we had a light again that the salt cellar had fallen again into the corner, and broken itself. Then I found out that the candle was not in the candlestick, and asked where it was. I told the girl to look for it, and then she felt among the things at the bottom of the stairs and picked up *three* candles, two of them quite new. We had only had *two* candles in the house [Mrs White expressly confirmed this – FP.], which had been bought just before and both had been partly burnt. I lit the old ones and left the new ones on the table; but they both disappeared afterwards, and I have never seen them since.

When the candle was lit again, I saw the little china woman jump off from the mantelpiece, and go into the same corner. It fell on its side, and then righted itself, and stood upright, unbroken. I distinctly saw it go through the air; it passed near to me as I stood about the middle of the room. None of us were near the mantlepiece. I picked it up, and presently it fell into the corner again, and broke itself. Then the tea caddy and the candlestick, all from the mantelpiece, followed. Then I went out and found George Ford ('Buck' Ford) and asked him to fetch Dr Lloyd for the child – for they had told me that all this disturbance mean the death of the child, who was very ill with an abscess in its back.

Then I got my wife to take the little lad out, and lay him next door, he lying on the squab in the kitchen at the time. [Mrs W. denied this, and said he was in the inner room – FP.] Rose went with her, and they took all the children with them. Before going, Rose had to go into the inner room, and then things began to fly about there and make a disturbance. All had been quiet there before.

I went after the others into the next house and stayed there some little time. When I came back, I found Police Constable Higgs in the kitchen. He and I were alone. (Rose all this time was next door). We heard a crash in the inner room, and we went in – Solomon Wass and Tom, who had just entered, with us, and Higgs with his lantern – and we found the chest of drawers turned up on end, and the lustres and looking glass, and everything else that had been on it, in pieces on the floor. Then we came back into the kitchen, and we saw the cupboard door open, and a big glass jar flew out, and flew into the yard and broke itself. Also some things flew off the bin at the side of the door, from the end near the fire; and they pitched in the corner, and then went out in the yard. Things often pitched on the floor by the door first, and then got up again and flew out into the yard.

Then Dr Lloyd came in with my wife, and Higgs showed him what had happened in the inner room. Then when we had got into the kitchen again, and were all standing near the door of the inner room – Higgs, my wife, and Tom, and Wass, and Lloyd – who was about six feet from the bin, and the nearest to it of our party – we all saw a basin which was lying on the bin near the door, get up two or three times in the air, rising slowly a few inches or perhaps a foot, and then falling plump. [Mrs W. corroborated this, and so did Mr Wass, the next-door-neighbour, who was also present – FP.] Then it got higher, and went slowly, wobbling as it went, up to the ceiling, and when it reached the ceiling, it fell down all at once, and broke itself.[3] Dr Lloyd then looked in the bin, saying the devil must be in the house, and then left. All the others shortly afterwards left, Mrs W., Rose and the children stopping in the next house. Tom and I sat in the chair on either side of the fire until the next morning at 8 a.m. Things kept on moving every now and then until about 2 a.m., and then all was quiet, and we got to sleep a bit. At about 8 a.m. I had to go out to see after a pig which had been pigging, and then things began again; and a lot of folks came in to see about it. Currass came in, and I went with him into the inner room and showed him the chest of drawers, he and I alone; we came out leaving the door open – I am quite sure it was open – and I was sitting near the fire, and Currass was just inside the kitchen, not far from the open door, when Wass's little lad, who was sitting at the table, said, ' There's the clock striking,' meaning the big clock which hung over our bed. I couldn't hear it, and said it was a lie. Just then we heard a crash, and I asked what it was, and Currass looked round and said it was the American clock had fallen right across the bed, and lay on the floor at the foot, with its bottom knocked out. Then I took it into the yard. I think – indeed, I am sure – that Coulter was *not* here when all this happened. The other clock fell and was broken, but whether before or after I cannot remember; and he may have seen that. I don't remember where the girl Rose was when the American clock fell. She may have been in the kitchen, but she certainly wasn't in the inner room; no one was in that room,

---

[3] During this scene the room was lighted by one candle, Higgs's lantern, and a blazing fire; so that the light was pretty good.

I am sure. I don't remember saying just at that time, though I often did say, that wherever she went the things smashed.

After that, Currass and I and one or two others were standing near to the outer door talking, when the china dogs, or one of them, flew off the mantelpiece and smashed; and lots of things kept on flying into the corner and smashing. I saw one of the dogs leave the mantelpiece and go through the air. I don't remember exactly when Coulter came; he may have been here when the china dog was smashed, but I don't remember that he was. Then a cream jug fell off the table; it had done so four or five times without smashing. At last I filled it with milk, and had placed it on the bin, when it suddenly fell off and smashed, and the milk was all spilt.

Then I was tired, and lay down on the squab; but things kept moving. I was told some pictures on the wall began to move, but I did not see them. At about 2 p.m. a Salvation Army woman came in and was talking to me as I lay on the squab; she stood near the inner door; Rose was near the outer door, having brought in some carpet. There were two candlesticks on the bin, at the end near the fireplace. Suddenly something dropped behind the Salvation Army woman. No one saw it going through the air; but we turned round and found that it was one of the brass candlesticks. It was half balanced on the small end where the candle goes, and was wobbling about on the end. Then the Salvation woman said, ' I must go,' and she went.

Then a little after, when Rose was going to lay down the carpet, and no one else in the room, a medicine bottle, full, fell from the bin on to the roll of carpet, about three or four yards off, and was broken. A lamp glass had fallen several times without breaking; but at last that fell and broke. Then an empty bottle flew off from the mantelpiece. That was one of the last things that happened. Well then, I couldn't stand it any longer. Wherever the lass seemed to go, things seemed to fly about. So I said to her, ' You'll have to go.' She began to roar. But my wife gave her some tea, and she went. That was between 4 and 5 p.m., very soon after the last disturbance. Nothing happened after she left. We sat up in the kitchen that evening, a lot of us, as the newspapers tell; but nothing happened at all.

I had been in the house three years. I think the house had been built four or five years before that. Nothing of the kind had ever happened in it before, as far as I know, except that once I thought I heard someone moving in the yard, and fancied it might be someone after the fowls; but there was no one there; and there was that strange tilting of the table when my wife was washing up the things about a week before.

The Wasses and the Willises [Mrs Willis is Wass's sister] had lived together in the next house; but since all these disturbances, the Willises have left the house; but Mr and Mrs Wass are still there.

(signed) Joseph White
New Building Ground, Worksop
8 April, 1883

Statement of Police Constable Higgs

(A man of good intelligence, and believed to be entirely honest. Fully alive, as becomes his official position, to White's indifferent reputation, but unable to account for what he saw – FP.)

On the night of Friday, 2 March I heard of the disturbances at Joe White's house from his young brother, Tom. I went round to the house at 11.55 p.m., as near as I can judge, and found Joe White in the kitchen of his house. There was one candle lighted in the room, and a good fire burning, so that one could see things pretty clearly. The cupboard doors were open, and White went and shut them, and then we came out and stood against the chest of drawers. I stood near the outer door. No one else was in the room at the time. White had hardly shut the cupboard doors when they flew open, and a large glass jar came out past me, and pitched in the yard outside, smashing itself. I didn't see the jar leave the cupboard, or fly through the air; it went too quick. But I am quite sure it wasn't thrown by White or any one else. White couldn't have done it without my seeing him. The jar couldn't go in a straight line from the cupboard out of the door; but it certainly did go.

Then White asked me to come and see the things which had been smashed in the inner room. He led the way and I followed. As I passed the chest of drawers in the kitchen I noticed a tumbler standing on it. Just after I passed I heard a crash, and looking round I saw that the tumbler had fallen on the ground in the direction of the fireplace, and was broken. I don't know how it happened. There was no one else in the room.

I went into the inner room, and saw bits of pots and things on the floor, and then I came back with White into the kitchen. The girl Rose had come into the kitchen during our absence. She was standing with her back against the bin near the fire. There was a cup standing on the bin, rather nearer the door. She said to me, 'Cup'll go soon; it has been down three times already.' She then pushed it a little further on the bin, and turned round and stood talking to me by the fire. She had hardly done so, when the cup jumped up suddenly about four or five feet into the air, and then fell on the floor and smashed itself. White was sitting on the other side of the fire.

Then Mrs White came in with Dr Lloyd; also Tom White and Solomon Wass. After they had been in two or three minutes, something else happened. Tom White and Wass were standing with their backs to the fire, just in front of it. Eliza Rose and Dr Lloyd were near them, with their backs towards the bin and the Doctor nearer to the door. I stood by the drawers, and Mrs White was by me near the inner door. Then suddenly a basin, which stood on the end of the bin near the door, got up into the air, turning over and over as it went. It went up not very quickly, not as quickly as if it had been thrown. When it reached the ceiling it fell plump and smashed. I called Dr Lloyd's attention to it, and we all saw it. No one was near it, and I don't know how it happened. I stayed about ten minutes more, but saw nothing else. I don't know what to make of it all. I don't think White or the girl could possibly have done the things which I saw.

(signed) William Higgs, G.E. 30
10 April 1883

Statement of Arthur Currass

(A coal miner; a Methodist, and apparently a very steady, respectable man. Believed that White did it, but couldn't guess how it was done – FP.)

I had to go out on the Saturday morning [3 March] to get some swill for the pig, about 8.15 a.m. I passed by White's house, and hearing a disturbance I looked over the railings, and White said to me, ' There's something in the house that's breaking all afore it '. I asked him what it were, and he told me to come and see. I got over the railings and I followed White into his own house. He took me into the front place where the clock was hanging over the bed's head, and was showing me a nest of drawers, where his suit of clothes came out of the bottom drawer into the top but one. While I was looking at the drawer, and the broken pots that was lying there, the clock by some means came from the wall, slantingwise about seven feet, and dropped clear of the bed's foot on to the floor. It had been fastened up on the wall, near the bed's head, and it fell between the bed's foot and the door. I said, ' What is that?' White said ' It's something else smashed.' I turned round and saw that it was the clock. The nail still remained in the wall. The girl Rose was coming out of the kitchen towards the inner door, but had not got quite up to it. She seemed to be much frightened. White said to me, ' It doesn't matter a damn where that lass goes, there's something smashes.' The clock was taken right away into the yard and placed on an empty cask, and there it stayed. White and I were alone in the front room when the clock fell. White and I then went into the back kitchen, and I remained about four feet from the outer door, with my face towards the fireplace. I then saw a pot dog leap up from the mantelpiece, and come within five feet of the pantry door and break, passing close to me. There was nothing attached to it, and there was no one near it. I then began to move away, and just then Coulter appeared. This would be between 8.30 and 8.45 a.m. Coulter did not come before whilst I was there, and certainly had not been present when the clock and the dog were broken. The clock was in the yard when he came, and I showed it him there.

(signed) Arthur Currass
John Street, Worksop
8 April 1883

I have given the evidence in this instance at considerable – perhaps tedious – length because, of all the cases which have been investigated by representatives of the Society, it is, as it stands, one of the most difficult to harmonize with any explanation by ordinary material causes. The concordant testimony of so many honest and fairly intelligent persons certainly produced, as will have been seen from my report, a strong impression on my mind at the time. Nor do I see any reason now to question my original estimate of their intelligence and good faith. If my verdict on the Worksop disturbances in 1896 differs from that which I gave in 1883, it is because many things have happened since that have taught me to discount testimony in matters of this kind.

For it will be seen that the value of these reports, as testifying to the operation of some supernormal agency, depends wholly upon two assumptions: first, that the various witnesses—imperfectly educated persons, not skilled in accurate observation of any kind – correctly described what they saw; and, second, that after an interval of more than five weeks, during which time the experiences had been discussed and compared and gaped at by every village fireside and in the public press, they correctly remembered what they described. But in the course of the thirteen years that have passed since I wrote my report we have received some striking object-lessons demonstrating the incapacity of the ordinary unskilled observer to detect trickery or sleight-of-hand; and we have learnt to distrust the accuracy of the unaided memory in recording feats of this kind, especially when performed under circumstances of considerable excitement.

And, indeed, if we scrutinize the account as it stands, we shall find various discrepancies and contradictions in the evidence. Thus (1) according to White, Higgs and he went into the front room first, to see the damage done there, and on their return to the kitchen a glass jar flew out of the cupboard; but according to Higgs's version, it was after seeing the glass jar fly through the air that White and he went into the inner room; (2) White's account is that two or three witnesses were present when the glass jar flew out; Higgs says, 'that no one else was in the room at the time '; (3) there seems to be a doubt as to whether Rose entered the kitchen during Higgs's visit: White does not mention her entrance at all; Higgs says they found her in the kitchen on their return from the inner room; (4) Currass says he was in the inner room on the morning of the third when the clock fell. White says that Currass was in the kitchen; (5) again, White cannot remember where Rose was at the time of the incident, while Currass says that she was near the inner door; (6) White and Currass agree that Coulter was not present when the American clock fell and was smashed; now Coulter, whom I saw, and who impressed me favourably as an honest man, stated that he was present when the clock fell, and also during the immediately succeeding disturbances in the kitchen.

Such are some of the discrepancies that appear even in evidence prepared and taken down from the lips of the witnesses by a too sympathetic reporter. It is probable that more and more serious discrepancies and contradictions would have been found if there had been no speculation and consultation and comparison in the interval of five weeks; and if each witness at the end of that time had written an independent account of the incidents.

It would be idle, in the circumstances and at this distance, to speculate on the real cause of these disturbances. But it is to be noted that Eliza Rose – the daughter of an imbecile mother – was present, by all accounts, at most of the disturbances; that they began shortly after her entrance to the cottage and ceased with her departure; and that she was regarded by White himself as the prime cause of all that happened. And if one apparently honest witness could describe himself as having seen occurrences that he knew of only by hearsay; if others could be mistaken as to the sequence of important events, and the presence or absence at given times of particular persons, it is perhaps not unreasonable to conjecture that the statements made by White and others that some abnormal movements took place during Rose's absence may have been incorrect, and that Rose herself, as the instrument of mysterious agencies, or simply as a half-witted girl gifted with abnormal cunning and love of mischief, may have been directly responsible for all that took place.

The Worksop Case is one of a number of poltergeist cases discussed by Frank Podmore in volume twelve of the *Proceedings* of the SPR, 1896-7. It will be noticed that Podmore, although puzzled by the undoubtedly strange happenings in the house, had reservations about the value of the evidence given by various witnesses. A man of acute intelligence, he was too critical of the standards of human observation for some of his contemporaries in the SPR, such as Andrew Lang, but it is this sceptical approach to the value of human testimony that has made him such a respected figure to modern writers on psychical research. His *Modern Spiritualism* (Methuen), in two volumes, although published as long ago as 1902, is still the standard work on the subject.

However, we must bear in mind, as some critical writers on psychical research are apparently not prepared to do, that discrepancies in the evidence of witnesses appear in a much wider field than that of parapsychology without totally invalidating the conclusions that may be drawn from such evidence. There are discrepancies in various accounts in the Gospels, discrepancies in accounts of even the simplest case which comes before the Courts of Justice, and discrepancies in accounts of trained observers of a battlefield. I need not labour this point. What, surely, we should do is to assess the evidence in a judicial manner, try to separate the important from the trivial, and take into consideration the character, intelligence and motive of the witnesses.

One of the strangest incidents concerned the basin which rose in the air, 'turning over and over as it went', until it reached the ceiling, after which it fell and was smashed. Police Constable Higgs said : 'I called Dr Lloyd's attention to it, and we all saw it. No one was near it and I don't know how it happened.' Some attention should obviously be paid to an incident witnessed by a policeman and a doctor together, since both are trained in exact observation.

I am not surprised that Dr A. R. G. Owen remarks in *Can We Explain the Poltergeist?* : 'A review of Podmore's cases rehabilitates the Worksop Case as genuine and well attested.' In his *Psychical Research Today* (Duckworth), first published in 1954, Dr D. J. West, says, 'It is doubtful if there are any poltergeists in which supernormal physical phenomena really take place. There has scarcely been anything approaching a convincing case published by the SPR in the last half century, although many scores of poltergeists have been investigated. One has to go back to such an instance as the Worksop Case, investigated by Frank Podmore of the SPR in 1883, to find any really challenging testimony.'

Readers may well be waiting with some impatience for something more about Eliza Rose (Rose was the girl's surname), 'the daughter of an imbecile mother', who, according to White, was the prime cause of all that happened. Podmore describes her as 'half-witted', speculates that she may have been gifted with abnormal cunning and love of mischief, but tells us nothing more of importance about her, not even her age. I hoped that a search of the archives of the SPR would yield information about the girl but there is nothing. This is a great pity. If we knew as much about Eliza Rose as we do about Virginia Campbell, the central figure in the Sauchie Case, we would be on firmer ground than we are at present in speculating on the possible causation of the strange events at Worksop.

15

The Haunting of Lew House

SABINE BARING-GOULD

[A long account of the haunting of Lew House, near Tavistock, Devon, is given by the Rev. Sabine Baring-Gould, author of the hymns 'Onward! Christian Soldiers' and 'Now the day is over', in his book *Early Reminiscences* (Hutchinson 1923). Baring-Gould, who died in 1924 at the age of ninety, was prolific in more ways than one. He wrote literally dozens of books, and was the father of fifteen children. Lew House was his family home. It was said to be haunted by the apparition of 'Old Madame', Margaret Belfield, the daughter of John Belfield, serjeant-at-law, who married William Drake Gould in 1740. Her husband died at Lew Trenchard in 1766 and after the death of her son Edward, who was unmarried, she took over the management of the property with conspicuous success. Madame Gould died on 10 April 1795.]

I may now give some of the ghost stories relative to Old Madame picked up by me as a boy, and happily written down by me as received.

There is a long corridor extending upstairs from the main staircase at the west end to the secondary flight at the east end. Along this a White Lady has been supposed to walk at night.

Murray, in his handbook of Devon, says: 'N.W. of Lydford is Lew Trenchard, so named from the family which at one time held it; but before the close of the seventeenth century it became the property of the Goulds, an ancient race which is honoured by the attendance of a true "White Lady". This is held to be the spirit of a certain Madame Gould; but she appears always in white, with long hair, and sparkling as if covered with water drops. She haunts the avenue of the old house, and was often seen in a long gallery which has been pulled down.' There are several inaccuracies in this account. We came into the property at the beginning, not the close of the seventeenth century; and the gallery has not been pulled down; it was divided up into three bedrooms by my father, but is now restored to its original condition.

My mother has often told me how she heard the steps at night, as though proceeding from high-heeled shoes, walking slowly along the corridor, and, thinking it might be my father coming to bed, she has opened the door to admit him; but on looking out she has seen the light through the windows illuminating the gallery down which she heard the measured tread, but could discern no person. On one occasion she followed these steps. They led into a room at the western extremity, which is now the boudoir, but she saw no one.

My sister frequently expressed her desire to hear the steps of the spectral lady and was disappointed, though she sat up on purpose. One summer night, however, she was sitting in her room, with window and door open, writing a letter and thinking of anything but the Old Madame, when she heard steps along the corridor. At the moment she thought it must be my father, and she rose, took up her candle and went to the door to speak to him, as she supposed he would scold her for sitting up so late. To her surprise she saw no one, but the steps passed her, and went on to the lumber room, now boudoir. Being a resolute and courageous young lady, she followed the sound into the room, but could see no one. She also opened the only other door beyond her own, which gave admission to one of the servants' apartments, to ascertain whether the noise could have proceeded thence; but found the two maids fast asleep.

RATS – that is my explanation of the tread along the gallery.

Barbara [Baring-Gould's eighth child, born in 1880], now Mrs L. F. Burnard, used to say as a child that she often saw a lady in *blue* who would visit the nursery, stoop over her, look at her, and sometimes sit beside her bed.

When Diana [his ninth child, born in 1882], now Mrs H. M. Batten, was dangerously ill, we had a trained nurse to attend her. One night the nurse had dozed off, when a tap came at the door, and a female voice said: 'It is time for her to have her medicine'. The nurse started up, ran to the door and opened it. No one was there, and my wife had not gone to warn the nurse. Another servant doubtless.

When little Beatrice [born in 1874] was ill, cutting teeth and with whooping cough, I did not think that the nurse-girl was sufficiently alert to attend to her, and so advised my wife to go into the bedroom, and sleep with Beatrice. I was then in the room in which Old Madame died, above the drawing-room. I was awoken about the middle of the night by my wife, who came in and said: 'I cannot sleep. I hear people tramping, carrying something down the stairs.'

I sat up and argued with her. It was a windy night, and the noise might be caused by the gale. As I was speaking there sounded three heavy strokes as if made by a clenched fist against the partition between the bedroom and the dressing-room.

'It is only the starting of the timber,' said I, and I induced my wife to go back to her bed.

Next day, so little did we think that Beatrice was in a serious condition, that we went off to make a call in Launceston. On our return I was sitting in the drawing-room, and my wife fetched the child, who was dressed, and took her down into the library. I heard a cry, and ran in, and found that the child had died on her mother's knees. Her coffin was carried down the staircase, as my wife had heard on the night before her death.

In 1918, the last year of the war, my youngest daughter Grace [born 1891], Mrs Calmady-Hamlyn, with her two children and a couple of nurses came to live with me at Lew, as her husband was in Palestine and Syria. Both nurses gave notice. They had been frightened by seeing a female form at night walking in the nursery, and stooping over the beds of the children. After that she engaged a superior Swiss nurse, who saw nothing – not being able to hear the tales of the *revenant* told by the other domestics.

Mrs Sperling, now of Coombe Trenchard, which was the old rectory, had her brother staying with her, Alister Grant, son of the Hon. A. Grant of Grant. He did much fishing in Lew water. We had then a very pretty governess, Miss Wilson, and Alister Grant was much smitten with her. One night he went to Lew Mill to see how the pheasants were getting on that the keeper was rearing, and sat on chatting with the keeper till late. As he returned along the road at the rear of the Avenue, parallel with it, and the moon was full, he saw a figure of a woman in white or grey, he could not say which, walking in the Avenue. Thinking it might be Miss Wilson, he leaned over the low wall, and spoke to her : but the figure passed between the boles of the tree. He spoke again – but there was no answer. Then it occurred to him that we were away at Bude, and that Miss Wilson was also away for her holiday. He became frightened, and ran as fast as his legs would carry him, till he had passed Lew House. He knew well enough that not one of our servants would venture to walk in the Avenue at night.

In 1877, a friend of mine, Mr Keeling, a solicitor at Colchester, was staying with me at Lew. He was sitting one evening in the settle, and I was in the arm-chair opposite him, in the hall. It was night and late. All at once we heard a sound of steps issuing from the door into what is now the ballroom, behind the settle, walking the length of the hall, with a dragging sound as of a trailing silk or satin dress. We both heard it. Keeling sprang to his feet and exclaimed: 'Good God! What is that?' I remained standing, for I also had risen, and thinking that possibly a drift of rain had swept the window, I ran to the door, opened it and looked out at the pavement before the window: it was perfectly dry.

On the confines of Orchard is a gloomy valley, called the Deep Way, through which trickles a rill of water, under the shadow of a plantation and wood. The Bratton–Clovelly road plunges into it – it is the ancient Via Regia – crosses a little bridge, and scrambles up the opposite side through the gloom of the overhanging trees. The gradient recently has been reduced by cutting down the hill and raising the road over the stream. On the side of the highway is an old mine-shaft, formerly some seven feet above the road, now level with it, and filled up. It is, or rather was, confidently asserted by Lew and Bratton people that on dark nights Madame Gould was to be seen, dressed in white, standing by the side of the stream, and that she stooped and took up handfuls of water, which she allowed to trickle down in sparkling drops through her fingers. Sometimes she combed her long flowing hair with a silver comb; and many a Bratton man, *returning from market*, had seen her and has been nearly frightened out of his wits by her.

In 1864, my wife and I drove over, by invitation, to have a high tea with the rector of Bratton, Rev. E. Seymour, and his wife and family. There was some difficulty about the meal, and Mrs Seymour had to apologize. Her cook had struck. She said that she would neither boil the kettle nor cook anything for us, as Old Madame had been the cause of her brother breaking his leg. As he was returning from Tavistock at night he had seen Old Madame at the mouth of the mine-shaft, all in white; and in his alarm, he had scrambled over the opposite hedge and had fallen and broken his leg. *Nota bene* – there are two public houses between Tavistock and Lew Down: till recently there were *three*.

A young man named Symonds, living at Holdstrong, but who had kinsfolk at Galford, left home for America during Madame Gould's life. After some years he returned, and hiring a horse at Tavistock he rode to Galford. It was a clear, moonlight night, and as he rode through the Lew Valley he noticed to the left of the road a newly ploughed field, in which a plough was standing. On this was seated a lady in white satin, with long hair flowing over her shoulders. Her face was uplifted and her eyes were directed towards the moon, so that Mr Symonds had a full view of it. He recognized her at once, and taking off his hat called out, ' I wish you a very good night, Madame'. She bowed in return, and waved her hand. The man noticed the sparkle of her diamond rings as she did so. ' She wears her years marvellously', thought Mr Symonds.

On reaching Galford, after the first greetings and congratulations, he said to his relatives: ' What do you think? I have seen that strange Madame Gould sitting on a plough, this time of night, looking at the moon'.

All who heard him stared, a blank expression passed over their countenances.

' Madame,' they said, 'was buried seven days ago in Lew Church.'

I heard this story from Mr Symonds of Holdstrong, and it was confirmed by those at Galford.

Mr Symonds of Holdstrong was wont to affirm that the old Madame walked nightly between Galford and Warson over Galford Down, passing through Holdstrong farm, by the old Church path and beside a dew pond on the down. Symonds said that he had never actually seen her, but that over and over again he had heard the rustle of her garments as she passed him. She had been seen by some of the men at Galford standing beside the dew pond for a moment and then sweep over the water and on her way. Doubtless the fog that gathers over the water and replenishes the pool.

A woman who entered the orchard, seeing the trees laden with apples, shook some down and filled her pockets, keeping one in her hand to eat. She turned to the gate into the road, and suddenly there flashed before her in the way the figure of Old Madame in white, pointing to the apple. The poor woman, in an agony of terror, cast it away and fled across the orchard to another exit, a gap, where a slate slab formed a bridge across the stream; but the moment she reached it, the figure of the White Lady appeared standing before the bridge, looking at her sternly and pointing to her pocket. It was not till the old goody had emptied it of the stolen apples, that the spectre vanished. This woman I knew: her name was Patience Kite, and she often told me the story, and assured me of its truth. [This experience related to the time when she was a girl.]

A carpenter who was employed to effect the alteration of Lew Church in 1832 worked late; he was alone, and before leaving one evening, out of curiosity, opened the vault or grave in the church, in which had been laid William Drake Gould and his lady.

Finding the lady's coffin-lid loose, he proceeded to raise it that he might take a look at the redoubted Madame. Immediately she opened her eyes, sat up and rose to her feet. The carpenter, an elderly man, frightened out of his wits, ran from the church, which was filled with light from the risen lady. As the man darted down the churchyard avenue, he turned his head back, and over his shoulder saw her gleaming in the porch and preparing to sail down the path after him. He lived in the Dower House – or rather in part of it, at Lew Mill, and the road passes nearly all the way through woods. He ran as he had never run before, and as he ran, so he told me, his shadow went before him, cast by the light that shone from the spectral lady that followed him. On reaching his house, he burst the door open and dashed into the bed beside his wife, who was infirm and bedridden. Both of them saw the figure standing in the doorway, and the light from it was so intense that, to use the old woman's words, she could have seen a pin lying on the floor.

We gave a ball on the occasion of my second daughter, Margaret's coming out [she was born in 1870]. When callers came after the ball, several of them asked who was that strange lady in a dark dress with lace, and grey hair, whom they had seen, who spoke to no one, and was addressed by no one. One gentleman said that he saw her standing under the portrait of Margaret Belfield, and he was struck with the resemblance, though the strange lady was older. The likeness was so great that he thought the lady must be a relation. There was no old lady at the ball.

A friend of mine, R. Twigge, was staying with me, and one evening he came down dressed for dinner, and opened the side door into the drawing-room, where he was surprised to see in the arm-chair with his back to him an old gentleman with either a white wig or with powdered hair, and opposite him an elderly lady in satin. He drew back surprised, and went round through the dining-room, and asked who those persons were in the drawing-room. I went at once in through the door into the hall, and found that the room was empty. The two figures were seen occupying the seats on opposite sides of the fireplace where once sat Parson Elford and old Madame Gould on Saturday and Sunday evenings.

My own impression is that there had been a transfer of the White Lady from Susanna Gould to Madame Gould. On 19 March 1729 Peter Trustcott, Gent., of Lew Trenchard, son of the rector, John Trustcott, married Susanna, daughter of Henry Gould of Lew Trenchard and Elizabeth his wife. There had been differences between the squire and the rector, political, I believe, as Henry was a strong Jacobite and Trustcott was a

Whig. Henry Gould strongly disliked the idea of this marriage, and it was probably due to trouble consequent on this that Susanna on her way back from the church to the house dropped down dead – in her bridal white – and was buried on 23 March. She had been forgotten, and the spectral form was transferred to Old Madame, who had no real claim to be seen in white.

Baring-Gould comments that as a boy he had talks with an old woman named Betsy Baker who remembered Madame Gould. When she died the shutter of the house flew open, and the hind [farmworker] who was in the kitchen, thinking there must be burglars breaking in, ran forth and saw Madame Gould standing by the walnut tree at the back of the house.

Baring-Gould's account may be read on two levels. One concerns tales to which little credence may be given, such as the one about the carpenter who disturbed the coffin of the redoubtable Madame and was chased by her all the way home. Indeed some elements of folklore may be discerned in certain stories. Baring-Gould took a great interest in folklore, and in *A Book of Folk Lore*, after giving the story of a lady in white being seen on a plough by a man who had returned from America, he says: 'I have troubled the reader with this story only because I think the incident of sitting on the plough is important as connecting the White Lady of Lew Trenchard with Frî, the Anglo-Saxon goddess.' It is understandable that stories about a remarkable woman should be passed round among country folk who were largely uneducated. Baring-Gould points out that in church Old Madame and the clerk were the only members of the congregation who could read, so that when a Psalm was given out the clerk said: 'Let Madame and I sing to the praise and glory of God.' In church she would stand up, look round to see who was there, and take count of those who were absent. The absentees were sure to hear of it in the week from her.

On the other level the stories may be considered as those to which Baring-Gould attached credence but which, he thought, were capable of a rational explanation – rats as a cause of foot-steps in the gallery; the number of public houses on a certain stretch of road as giving opportunities for drinking, and hence flights of imagination; the probability that it was a servant, and not a ghostly voice, who gave warning that it was time that Diana should have her medicine – and others in which he was personally involved.

For instance, he was awakened by his wife who said she could not sleep because of the sound of people tramping and carrying something down the stairs. It was then that he heard the sound of three heavy strokes against the partition. The next day little Beatrice died and her coffin *was* carried down the stairs. It may be argued that it was just coincidence that the child died at that time, but if so it was a remarkable one; the death was not expected.

There are some similarities between this case and the haunting of Cleve Court, in Kent, which I discussed in *The Unexplained*. In both there was the sound of footsteps as if made by a woman wearing high-heeled shoes. There were knocks on the door at Cleve Court and at Lew House.

The Rev. Bickford H. C. Dickinson, Baring-Gould's grandson and author of an excellent book *Sabine Baring-Gould* (David and Charles 1970), was told by an elderly American lady, a great friend of the family, that she had heard footsteps coming down the long gallery. They stopped at her door and were followed by knocking.

'But,' she said seriously, 'I had the presence of mind not to say "Come in".' She was quite convinced that Old Madame was far too polite to come in uninvited.

Several people at the coming-out ball of Miss Margaret Baring-Gould saw an elderly woman who resembled the Mar-garet Belfield of the portrait (Old Madame in her younger days), but she spoke to no one and was addressed by no one. Readers of *The Unexplained* will remember the child at Cleve Court who referred to the 'poor lady' who 'walks in and out. No one speaks to her and no one tells me who she is.'

Baring-Gould told how a guest of his saw an old gentleman with either a white wig or with powdered hair sitting opposite an elderly lady in satin. This was in the drawing-room, and the seats they occupied on opposite sides of the fireplace were those where once Parson Elford and old Madame Gould sat on Saturday and Sunday evenings. When Baring-Gould went into the drawing-room it was empty. This incident reminds me of the one related by Mrs Norma E. Davies, of Sheffield, which is included in *Apparitions and Ghosts*. One night in 1967 she came downstairs to get medicine for her sick son and saw in the living-room the figure of her dead father and uncle conversing noiselessly. When she returned with her husband they had gone.

A stream ran close to Lew House and Baring-Gould does not seem to have considered that the sounds that he interpreted as footsteps might have been caused by the noise of water conducted upwards by pipes. This stream is now dry, Mr Dickinson tells me. He is a former rector of Lew Trenchard, as was his celebrated grandfather. Lew House is now an hotel.

I will close this account of the haunting of Lew House with details of a crisis apparition given by Sabine Baring-Gould in his *Early Reminiscences*.

On 3 January 1840, at night, my mother was sitting reading her Bible in the dining-room at Bratton [Bratton Clovelly, near Lew Trenchard] when, looking up, she saw on the further side of the table, the form of her brother Henry who was in the Navy serving in the South Atlantic. She looked steadily at him, and there was a kindly expression on his face; but presently the apparition faded. She has told me that she realized at once what this meant, and she made an entry in pencil on the fly-leaf at the end of the Bible :

Saw Henry, 3 January 1840. It was not till over a month that the news reached Exeter that he had died on that very date off Ascension. His brother, Commander Francis Godolphin Bond, died at sea near St Helena, 16 July 1840. I never heard my mother say that she had seen an apparition of this brother.

If the Bible in which Baring-Gould's mother made her entry could be found it would provide an excellent piece of evidence.

16

A Family Ghost

OSBERT SITWELL

[When the late Sir Osbert Sitwell, one of the finest writers of our time, was compiling the introduction to the first volume of his autobiography, *Left Hand Right Hand!* (Macmillan 1952), he did so in a room in Renishaw, his seat in Derbyshire, within three miles of which his family had lived for at least seven hundred years.

His great-great-grandfather was Sir Sitwell Sitwell, tall and well-built, who was described by Sir Osbert as a man of impulsiveness, high spirits, taste, audacity and temperament. His existence was chiefly divided between sport and building. One of the strangest of his exploits was to kill with his hounds a 'Royal Bengal Tiger' which had escaped from a menagerie in nearby Sheffield in November 1798. He added very largely to Renishaw, specially erecting the ballroom for a rout he gave to the Prince of Wales in 1806. Sir Sitwell died of gout in the head at the early age of forty-two.]

Now we turn to Sir Osbert's account in *Left Hand Right Hand!* :

Mrs Swinton, in *Two Generations* [edited by Osbert Sitwell, Macmillan 1940] describes how Sir Sitwell was twice seen after his death, once in the streets of Sheffield, and once – on the same night – at Renishaw, while his body was still lying in the library. It was a very silent evening, after dark, and a relative of his widow's was sitting in the hall, next to the room in which was the coffin. She heard a ring at the front-door bell and, the servants being at supper, opened the door herself. Sir Sitwell, his face illuminated by the lamp she held up, looked steadily at her from the darkness beyond and then disappeared. . . . The same incident, or something akin to it, has happened on more than one occasion; the face of a man, for example, was seen looking through the door at the time of the funeral of Sir George, Sir Sitwell's son, some forty years later. . . . These singular stories possess for me an especial interest, because on the evening of the day on which I first heard of my mother's fatal illness, I entered the house, having returned from an expedition to Bolsover, to find two friends, who were staying with me at the time, much puzzled because a tall, rather indistinct figure had mounted the steps from the park and stared at them through the identical glass panels of the door; but when they opened it, he was no longer there, nor anywhere to be seen.

Let us now turn back to the original narrative from which Sir Osbert quotes. The Mrs Swinton, of *Two Generations,* was Georgiana Caroline Sitwell, born on 31 August 1824, the third of the five daughters of Sir George and Lady Sitwell. She married in 1856 Archibald Campbell Swinton of Kimmerghame as his second wife. Here is her own account:

A strange story is told of Sir Sitwell's appearance at Renishaw on the night previous to his own funeral. The body had lain for several days in the library, and the house was steeped in the silence usual on such solemn occasions. My grandfather's half-sister, Mrs Margaret Stovin, was sitting alone in the hall and heard a faint ring at the front door. The servants had gone for their supper, and, unwilling to disturb them, she took up a lamp and went to the door herself. On opening it she saw (as she thought) Sir Sitwell. He looked her full in the face, then turned and disappeared in the darkness. The same night he was reported to have been seen in the streets of Sheffield. Some supposed that the figure must have been that of Frank, Sir Sitwell's brother. He had quarrelled shamelessly with Sir Sitwell; and the explanation may be that remorse, or some lingering spark of feeling, had made him wish to see in death the brother he had injured, and to be present at the funeral; but that, entertaining an aversion for all the Stovin connection, when he had encountered Mrs Margaret at the door, his good resolutions had vanished and he had fled from her presence.

Before we consider these two accounts we may turn to what Sir Osbert considered was an experience with a ghost, when he was a very young child. He says in *Left Hand Right Hand!* :

At Scarborough the night nursery was at the top and back of the high old stone-pillared house we then occupied. . . . At the time of which I write, people still scarcely existed for me; the cry, the song, the tune on the barrel-organ, but not those who uttered or produced them. Indeed, it is a question that I did not see and remember a ghost before I could pin down any human being in my mind, since a giant and spectral figure was seen one summer morning, just as it was growing light, a figure, immense, gaunt and grey like a shadow, that rushed round the room, its rhythm faster and faster, but making no sound. . . . We all saw it, my nurse, my sister and myself – or so it was supposed, for I first called the attention of my two sleeping companions to it, by yelling, loud and long. Our nurse got up, and the figure, nine or ten feet high, rushed like a wind through the door, which it must have left open, into nothingness, no sound, no trace, no sign. There was no one there, and I have no solution to the mystery to offer. The event, or the hallucination, or whatever it may have been, remains inexplicable. Yet I will not dismiss it from its early place of honour in my life for fear of not being believed. . . . So it was, as far as the three of us could tell.

It is possible that what the two children and the nurse saw was a mist figure. These are occasionally seen indoors. A vortex is liable to form in the atmosphere, especially in summer, with a resulting drop in temperature in the centre of it, causing water vapour there to condense to the point of visibility and to produce a grey 'spectral' figure, sometimes of superhuman height.

Let us now consider Mrs Swinton's account of the figure seen at the time of the death of Sir Sitwell Sitwell. Mrs Stovin saw, as she thought, Sir Sitwell, but 'some supposed that the figure must have been that of Frank, Sir Sitwell's brother'. We do not know if Frank Sitwell resembled his brother but Mrs Stovin certainly did know, and she identified the figure as that of Sir Sitwell. However, allowances must be made for the possibility that her lamp did not cast a very clear light and she was mistaken in her identification. There still remains to be explained the incidents in which the face of a man was seen looking through the door at the time of the funeral of Sir George, Sir Osbert's great-grandfather, and the tall man who looked at Sir Osbert's friends through the glass panels of the door. It may be argued that these figures were those of strangers who went quickly away, but I am far from convinced that this is the answer to the puzzle.

There is a parallel case to the accounts of the 'peering man' at Renishaw in volume three of *Proceedings* of the SPR. This concerns a woman, her husband and stepdaughter and two small children, with servants, who lived in a detached house which was not more than twenty years old. The woman was playing the piano about eleven o'clock one morning when she was suddenly aware of a figure peeping round the corner of the folding doors to her left. Thinking it must be a visitor, she jumped up and went into the passage, but no one was there, and the hall door, which was half glass, was shut. She saw only the upper half of the figure, which was that of a tall man with a very pale face and moustache. Another time she was playing cricket in the garden with her little boys when she saw the same face peeping round at her out of the kitchen door.

Sir Osbert was a member of the Society for Psychical Research. No doubt his interest in psychical research was stimulated by a faculty he apparently had for precognitive dreams. Once he dreamt correctly beforehand a winning number at the roulette table :

In my sleep a voice said to me, 'Back the number fifteen when the casino clock is at the hour.' The following afternoon I went into the rooms and a little later, seeing that the minute hand of the clock marked the hour – six o'clock – precisely as the ball was thrown, I hurriedly did as I had been bidden, and put on all the money I had brought with me. . . . And, I won! On other occasions, too, I have dreamed of events that were subsequently to occur, though these were not so pleasant. . . .

However, this is a book about ghosts, not about dreams that come true, so there we must leave Sir Osbert and the strange events at Renishaw.

17

The Return

L. A. G. STRONG

[Among the friends whom the future author made at Brighton College was Vincent Morris, a boy with a lively sense of humour of the gambolling, ebullient kind. He was deeply religious, and popular with the other boys. Strong went on to Wadham College, Oxford, and Morris into the Forces. This account was written in the spring of 1917.]

I had news that Vincent Morris had been wounded. We had been in continuous touch since he joined the Forces. A good correspondent, he kept me informed of his many adventures, and he finished up as a pilot. Flying delighted him. . . . His religious beliefs had deepened with the experiences of war, without damage to the violent gaiety and sense of the ridiculous which had distinguished him at school. In the short, dedicated time after he left Brighton, he managed to meet and overcome his weaknesses in a series of dramatic encounters, which I am not entitled to set down here; and it was very much in his pattern that, when his plane was shot down, it narrowly missed in its fall a famous statue of the Madonna which had been knocked horizontal but remained at the top of a ruined church tower.

Vincent's injuries were severe, and the surgeons amputated a leg; but there seemed every hope of his recovery, and I had a cheerful letter from him, saying that he expected to be back in his beloved garden at Ashbourne, where I had more than once been his guest, in time to see the roses. After some days, however, he grew worse and the surgeons saw that they would have to amputate the other leg. Vincent's parents and sisters were sent for. They sat with him for an hour in the morning, leaving before lunch-time; the operation was to take place at two. He was very tired when they said good-bye, and one of his sisters, turning in the doorway for a last look, saw him sigh and close his eyes. When two o'clock came, the operation was not even begun, for he died almost immediately after going under the anaesthetic.

We had made a pact at school that whoever died first should try to appear to the other. Because of this pact, for the first ten days I was jumpy, on the lookout for him. The feeling was apprehension, rather than fear. Stage fright is the nearest I can get to describing it. Nothing happened, however : by degrees I relaxed, and all questions of his possible appearance slipped from my mind.

But Vincent kept his promise. Three months later, when I was at home at Yelverton, in the early hours of one morning he came to my bedroom. Experiences like this are difficult to tell, and it is perhaps unwise to say even this much. In the nature of things I can bring no evidence, and the bare assertion means that those to whom such things are inadmissible must think I am deluded, or that I am trying to delude them. Yet, because the experience was as real to me as any in my life, and because, if it did not happen, I cannot be sure anything has ever happened to me which has not been corroborated by independent witness, I should be false to the major premiss of my life if I did not record it. . . .

Vincent made one further communication, dimmer and more fragmentary, at the following Christmas. I remembered after it had come that Christmas was for him a very special season, with deeper emotional connotations than for most people. . . .

[Strong, who died in 1958, took a great interest in psychical research. He carried out experiments in thought transference with Cecil Glenn, classics master at the Hoe Preparatory School, Plymouth.]

Something happened during the summer holiday which suggested that the deliberate practice of thought transmission may have formed a link between our minds that could work without any exercise of will. One afternoon, I was in the garden at Walmer Villa, lying in a deck chair and staring unseeingly past a great clump of lavender and the trees at the meadow's end to the houses and spire of Glenageary. Suddenly all this faded, and I saw instead a bay with a green headland dominated by a small white lighthouse. In the foreground was a sloping beach. Almost immediately, into the picture, which, though its edges were blurred, seemed like a cinema screen, Cecil Glenn walked, his back to me, towards the water, at an angle from right to left. He entered the water and swam towards some indeterminate black objects on the extreme left of my picture. He climbed out on these, yet I could not see what they were. They remained indistinct and fuzzy, and for a while I lost sight of him. Then he re-entered the water and began to swim back towards the shore; and I felt, rather than saw, that a current was flowing against him, and he was having a hard struggle. He took a long time to swim in, and at last scrambled out on all fours, exhausted.

When I met him at the beginning of the next term, I asked him about his holiday. He said he had spent some of the time in Cornwall.

'Did you bathe?' I asked him.

'I did,' he answered. 'One day I was damned near drowned.'

'Don't say a word,' I interrupted. 'I'll tell you about it,' and I repeated to him what I had seen.

He confirmed it exactly, filling in the one detail of which I had not been sure. The black objects on the left of my picture were a couple of small, tarred fishing boats, and he had managed to scramble out on one of them to rest himself. Later he had been told of the folly of bathing from that beach on a falling tide.

[Strong says, 'The experiments were unwise. On the mornings that followed, we would both have headaches, and I remember feeling ill and depleted.' He wrote for advice to Sir Oliver Lodge, whose book *Reason and Belief* had deeply impressed him. Sir Oliver introduced him to Professor F. C. S. Schiller, a fellow of Corpus and a well-known philosopher, who was president of the SPR in 1914. Strong carried out experiments in telepathy while under hypnosis with the professor and a friend of his named Girdlestone, but became frightened because of some of the results which followed.]

That the whole business was dangerous I soon found out. I do not want to say much about this, still less to describe experiences which came to me involuntarily, both alone and in company, after the experiments had been going on for some months. One reason for reticence is that to describe happenings so remote from common experience is to risk being thought a liar or a lunatic. Anyone who is conversant with extra-sensory phenomena will know the risks I was running, and realise that to open a door in this way is to encourage it to open of itself at times when there will be no control over what comes through it. There was little control in Schiller's rooms, apart from the presence of two honest and kindly men. When I was alone in my own rooms there was none at all.

An analogy may be useful to readers who have had no occasion to think about this subject. Most people have seen a slide-rule. Imagine that the length of the rule represents the entire universe, and the part contained by the small movable panel represents as much of the universe as we perceive through the senses. For the purpose of this illustration it does not matter where the movable slide is, provided that it is stationary some-where on the rule. The amount of the universe which we per-ceive through our senses is determined, roughly speaking, by our biological needs. That is only a small section we know through various aids to perception which enables us to be aware of more, and in greater detail. The point is that most human beings agree in the range of what they are able to see, feel, hear, etc., and that this range, this level of perception, is, like the area of the slide rule enclosed by the panel, a small part of the whole.

Now it is possible, by means of such experiments as I had been taking part in, and by other methods, slightly to shift one's level of perception; in terms of our illustration, slightly to move the sliding panel, so as to include within it things not normally perceived by the senses. A person to whom this has happened will be liable to see or hear, or even to touch, con-stituents of the universe which to normal people remain invisible and inaudible and intangible. Such experiences, unless he has been carefully prepared for them, may greatly disturb his peace of mind, if not unhinge him : and at the end of this progres-sion, stands the fact that a person whose view of reality is markedly different from that of his fellow creatures runs the risk of being carted off in a plain van.

Well; things happened to me when I was alone, and, on one melodramatic occasion, in a don's drawing-room on the Wood-stock Road, which were highly disturbing to my peace of mind. If *these* were the results of developed perceptions, I wanted none of them. There is a curious horror about experiences which are imperceptible to other people. They isolate one in a way hard to describe. Only those who have been through similar experiences can have any idea of the feelings of confusion and loneliness which they bring.

[Naturally, the experiments were discontinued. But Strong had a strange experience on a Sunday evening in the summer of 1921, when he was a master on the staff of Summer Fields, a preparatory school in North Oxford. Among the other masters was W. S. Case, a talented man, who for a few years was one of Strong's closest friends.]

An experience of these days when Case was at his peak must be recorded because I have never met another like it. . . . Service had just finished in the school chapel and I walked back to the Cottage. The front door led into a hall. Immediately on the left was Case's sitting room. He had not yet come out from chapel where he had been playing the organ. The hall ran through the house to the back door. My room was at the back, on the left, and John's [another master] on the right. Beside the back door, against the wall, was a cupboard where we kept our gowns.

I shut the hall door behind me, walked to the cupboard, opened it, took off my gown, and hung it on its peg. As I did this, I heard the hall door open behind me. I turned and saw a man with a brown moustache, carrying music under his left arm, come in, close the door, and go into Case's room. Case had a moustache, and would be carrying music, so, naturally enough, for the moment I took the figure to be Case.

Then, after a second to two, I realized that he was not Case. His clothes were different. His moustache was different. His whole look was different.

' Who on earth – ?' I thought : and I went into Case's room to see. There was no one there.

I stood, staring, incredulous. I had not only seen the man go in, I had heard him open the front door. It was the sound of the door that had made me turn from hanging up my gown.

A strange, slow tingle travelled up my spine. Outside, the summer evening was radiant over the well-known scene, the roof of the cottage opposite, the flowers, the lawn, the little gravel drive. Everything that I was looking at contradicted this sudden chill of the unexplained. Then in the gate came Case, his music under his arm, humming to himself. I met him in the doorway. He narrowed his eyes.

'Hullo! You look odd.'

'A very odd thing's happened.' I told him what I had heard and seen. 'Naturally,' I concluded, 'at first I thought it was you.'

He looked at me strangely through his glasses. 'What was he like?'

I gave him an exact description. As I was giving it, I marvelled that I had not instantly realized the stranger could not possibly have been Case.

Case turned away, and put his music down on the table. 'Oh,' he said over his shoulder, 'that was Winford Alington. He was killed in 1917. He played the organ here before me. This was his room.'

It would seem that somehow, for a couple of seconds, I had tuned in to the past and seen the figure of Case's predecessor at the exact hour when he must so often have come across from playing in the chapel, with his music under his arm. But – this is the point that interests me most – I not only saw him, I *heard* him open the door. Did that door physically open and shut? Did I hear a physical noise, or did I translate to hearing, as well as to sight, a stimulus from the past? Of one thing I am certain, and later experiences confirm my certainty. The spirit of the dead schoolmaster was not walking. I was, so to speak, playing a gramophone record; reconstituting by my perceptions an image from the past: seeing something which was not happening when I saw it, but had happened for the last time several years before. Did I go back to it? Did it come forward to me? Or did we meet halfway?

I have since had several experiences in which a detail from the past was re-enacted before my eyes, including one when I seemed to hear words spoken; but none in which my attention was first drawn by what appeared to be a physical sound coming from a material object.

The above extracts are taken from *Green Memory* by L. A. G. Strong (Methuen 1961). It is most interesting to note that in one book the late Mr Strong, a gifted and sensitive writer, shows that he takes two different views of apparitional experiences. For instance, he says of the incident concerning Vincent Morris that three months after his death 'in the early hours of one morning he came to my bedroom'. Although no details are given, it is obvious that Strong was deeply affected by the experience and for him his friend was actually in the room. It it worth noting that Strong thought his friend might appear to him after death, as a pact had been made between them that whoever died first should try to appear to the other, and that for quite a while he was apprehensive about this, but by degrees he relaxed 'and all questions of his possible appearance slipped from my mind'. It was only when Strong was sufficiently relaxed that he had the experience of what he regarded as the actual return of his friend. This is what one would expect from a study of apparitions. People who are keyed up to 'see' a ghost, as when they spend a night in an allegedly haunted house, are in too tense a state of mind for the experience to happen.

On the other hand, he says of his experience at Summer Fields that 'the spirit of the dead schoolmaster was not walking. I was, so to speak, playing a gramophone record. . . .' Strong was probably influenced in his views by the great Irish poet W. B. Yeats, whom he knew for the last twenty years of his life. Yeats took a great interest in psychical research, in the occult in general and also in magic. He believed that all material forms were interpretations put by our own senses upon eternal reality. 'True to his nature, he called them dramatizations.'

Yeats told Strong: 'No man has ever spoken to a spirit – what appears is a dramatization.' This view has something in common with that expressed in *Apparitions* by G. N. M. Tyrrell, who speaks of 'apparitional dramas' and 'the machinery employed to express them'.

Strong was intrigued by the experience at Summer Fields when he 'heard' a door being opened by an apparition. This led him to ask: 'Did I hear a physical noise, or did I translate to hearing, as well as to sight, a stimulus from the past?' Tyrrell, discussing the characteristics of apparitions, says that 'the apparition might pick up any object in the room or open and close the door. We should both see and hear these objects moved: yet physically they would never have moved at all.' If this view is correct, and I agree with it, the 'noise' of the door's opening which Strong heard was an auditory hallucination.

I was glad to have confirmation of Tyrrell's views in a letter I received from a correspondent, Miss Rachel Simmons. She wrote:

After my mother died, an aunt (my father's sister) came to look after us and keep house. The family were very keen that we should learn to play the piano and my elder sister and I were having lessons. In addition to our usual practising my sister and I were made to practise for about half an hour before breakfast every morning. As there was only one piano we had to take it in turns to do this. We were always alone in the drawing room but as we could be heard we were afraid to stop playing.

My aunt suffered from dyspepsia, also had a 'weak heart', and did not come downstairs quite so early, but when she did it was her invariable habit to open the door of the drawing room and say, (I cannot remember her exact words, but most probably) 'Good morning, dear'. Having said that she would shut the door and go downstairs to the dining room.

One morning I was practising at the piano when the door opened and I saw my aunt standing there dressed in her usual get-up and carrying in her hand a jug as usual (probably taken up earlier with hot water).

I was about to say 'Good morning' when I realized that she had disappeared and the door was shut, and stopped playing for an instant. Though I had seen the open door I knew that it had never been open, and though I had seen my aunt as she usually appeared, I knew that I had not really seen her, though she appeared to me as quite solid and real.

My aunt had not died, but she was feeling unwell that morning and did not come downstairs till later.

I was about ten when this happened.

Comparison may be made of the 'arrival' of the aunt with that of the nurse in the case related by Dr Margaret Murray.

Strong's account of the 'return' of Vincent Morris interests me greatly because it is similar to others in the literature of psychical research. The authors of *Phantasms of the Living* (1886) quote from the autobiographical *Life and Times of Lord Brougham* (1871) an account of how he saw the apparition of a friend with whom he had made a pact that the first who died would appear to the other. In December 1799 Lord Brougham was travelling in Sweden with friends.

We set out for Gothenburg apparently on December 18 determining to make for Norway. About one in the morning, arriving at a decent inn, we decided to stop for the night. Tired with the cold of yesterday, I was glad to take advantage of a hot bath before I turned in, and here a most remarkable thing happened to me – so remarkable that I must tell the story from the beginning.

After I had left the High School, I went with G., my most intimate friend, to attend the classes in the University. There was no divinity class, but we frequently in our walks discussed and speculated upon many grave subjects – among others, on the immortality of the soul, and on a future state. This question, and the possibility, I will not say of ghosts walking, but of the dead appearing to the living, were subjects of much speculation : and we actually committed the folly of drawing up an agreement, written with our blood, to the effect that whichever of us died the first should appear to the other, and thus solve any doubts we had entertained of the 'life after death'. After we had finished our classes at the college G. went to India, having got an appointment there in the Civil Service. He seldom wrote to me, and after the lapse of a few years I had almost forgotten him; moreover, his family having little connection with Edinburgh, I seldom saw or heard anything of them, or of him through them, so that all his schoolboy intimacy had died out, and I had nearly forgotten his existence. I had taken, as I said, a warm bath, and while lying in it and enjoying the comfort of the heat after the late freezing I had undergone I turned my head round, looking towards the chair on which I had deposited my clothes, as I was about to get out of the bath. On the chair sat G., looking calmly at me. How I got out of the bath I know not, but on recovering my senses I found myself sprawling on the floor. The apparition, or whatever it was, that had taken the likeness of G., had disappeared.

Lord Brougham wrote an account of the experience in his journal at the time. He said: 'No doubt I had fallen asleep; and that the appearance presented so distinctly to my eyes was a dream I cannot for a moment doubt.' The authors of *Phantasms of the Living* are dubious about this conclusion and shrewdly ask, 'Is it a well-known result of an ordinary dream that the dreamer on recovering his senses, finds himself "sprawling on the floor"?' I believe that Lord Brougham was unable to admit to himself that he had seen an apparition and therefore decided that the experience *must* have been a dream. Shortly after Lord Brougham returned to Edinburgh a letter from India conveyed the news that G. had died on 19 December. When Lord Brougham had the experience of 'seeing' his old friend he was tired after a long journey and was taking a warm bath. This almost certainly produced the drowsy relaxed state in which experiences of the type described in this book are apt to occur.

18

The Apparition in my Cabin

HAROLD OWEN

Towards the end of the First World War Harold Owen, painter
and writer, who died in his Oxfordshire home on 26 November
1971, was serving as an officer in the light cruiser HMS *Astraea*
in African waters. His elder brother Wilfred, later to become
famous as a war poet, was an Army officer on the western
front. On Armistice Day, 11 November 1918, the cruiser was
anchored in Table Bay. The captain invited all officers to his
day cabin for drinks to mark the cessation of hostilities. Harold
Owen, then twenty-one, said: 'I could not enter into any spirit
of gaiety. I felt horribly flat, everything else seemed flat.'
Apprehensive about the safety of his brother, he drafted a cable
of inquiry to his father in England and then tore it up. 'Was
Wilfred all right, was Colin [his younger brother]? I wish now
I *had* sent that cable. I could not be happy about any of them
at home. Something I knew was wrong. Monstrous depression
clamped hold of me.' Harold Owen was in this mood when the
cruiser sailed for Walfish Bay and the Cameroons.

In Victoria again, limp and enervated with the moist heat and
recurrent malaria, insects plagued us day and night. . . . I
found it difficult to throw off a lowness of spirits. Now that the
war was over it seemed less necessary to do so, which made it
harder. Malaria of course was doing its undermining work. It
may have been something to do with this unusually low state of
mind that I was going through which brought about for me
an extraordinary and inexplicable experience.

We were lying off Victoria. I had gone down to my cabin thinking to write some letters. I drew aside the door curtain and stepped inside and to my amazement I saw Wilfred sitting in my chair. I felt shock running through me with appalling force and with it I could feel the blood draining away from my face. I did not rush towards him but walked jerkily into the cabin – all my limbs stiff and slow to respond. I did not sit down but looking at him I spoke quietly : ' Wilfred, how did you get here?' He did not rise and I saw that he was involuntarily immobile, but his eyes which had never left mine were alive with the familiar look of trying to make me understand; when I spoke his whole face broke into his sweetest and most endearing dark smile. I felt no fear – I had not when I first drew my door curtain and saw him there; only exquisite mental pleasure at thus beholding him. All I was conscious of was a sensation of enormous shock and profound astonishment that he should be here in my cabin. I spoke again : ' Wilfred dear, how can you be here, it's just not possible. . . .' But still he did not speak but only smiled his most gentle smile. This not speaking did not now as it had done at first seem strange or even unnatural; it was not only in some inexplicable way perfectly natural but radiated a quality which made his presence with me undeniably right and in no way out of the ordinary. I loved having him there : I could not, and did not want to try to, understand how he had got there. I was content to accept him; that he was here with me was sufficient. I could not question anything, the meeting in itself was complete and strangely perfect. He was in uniform and I remember thinking how out of place the khaki looked amongst the cabin furnishings. With this thought I must have turned my eyes away from him; when I looked back my cabin chair was empty. . . .

I felt the blood run slowly back to my face and looseness into my limbs and with these an overpowering sense of emptiness and absolute loss. . . . I wondered if I had been dreaming, but looking down I saw that I was still standing. Suddenly I felt terribly tired and moving to my bunk I lay down; instantly I went into a deep oblivious sleep. When I woke up I knew with absolute certainty that Wilfred was dead. . . .

The certainty of my conviction of Wilfred's death amounted I realized to absolute knowledge; I could no longer question it. That I had not heard that he had been killed – that weeks had passed since the fighting had stopped – made no difference to me at all; all that could be explained. What I found impossible to explain was this self-existent awareness of mine, unrelated to any facts; I did not try. I accepted his death completely without hope and without pretence. My awareness was so profound that knowledge could not be denied. . . .

Throughout my whole being I felt moved as meaning stirred deeply within me. I became enriched with an accepting humility as recognition flooded into me that I had, for precious moments, known the lifting of a veil and with this been allowed to share an illuminating experience of unique significance and surpassing beauty. . . .

This extract is taken from volume three (*War*) of *Journey from Obscurity* by Harold Owen (Oxford University Press 1956).

The time factor in Harold Owen's experience of seeing the apparition of his brother is important. Wilfred Owen was killed on 4 November 1918, his family received 'the dreaded telegram' at twelve noon on 11 November, Armistice Day, and Harold Owen did not see the apparition in his cabin until some weeks after that; the date is not given. The period of latency of the experience is therefore unusually long. It may be presumed that conditions were not favourable until then : the noise and excitement of the Armistice Day celebrations, and the parties that would almost certainly follow on board ship, could result in an atmosphere being built up around the young lieutenant in which he never felt really alone.

What was persistent, however, was his feeling that something was wrong. The chapter containing the account given here starts: 'The last weeks of the war were for me extremely unhappy ones. I find it difficult to explain satisfactorily why this should have been so. Certainly there were no special happenings that might cause me to feel like this; it bothered me that I could not – to myself – account for my restless unease.' There are a number of cases in the literature of psychical research in which a feeling that something was wrong coincided with a death or illness of which the subject was unaware. I will give only one. It is from volume two of *Phantasms of the Living* and was supplied by Mrs Herbert Davy of Newcastle-on-Tyne in 1883.

It was in August, a few years ago – my husband was at the moors. I drove to a nursery garden to procure some flowers. I waited outside the gate under the shelter of some trees, sending the groom in for the flowers.

It was one of the hottest afternoons I ever experienced. My ponies, usually restive, stood perfectly still. Before I had waited there many minutes, an unaccountable feeling took possession of me as though I foresaw and recognized the shadow of coming sorrow. I immediately associated it with my husband – that some accident had befallen him. With this miserable apprehension upon me, I got through the day and evening as best I could, but weighed down by the shadow, though I spoke of it that night to no one.

Nothing had happened to my husband. But a little child – a relation who had lived with us and been almost as our own – had died that day rather suddenly in Kent, where she was then visiting her parents. . . .

In this case news of the death was received comparatively quickly. In the case concerning the death of Wilfred Owen his parents were not notified until a week later and his brother had still not been notified some weeks after the fighting had stopped;

the news of the death was conveyed, by implication, by the appearance of the apparition in Harold Owen's cabin.

In his presidential address to the SPR in 1966 Professor Sir Alister Hardy, FRS, quotes Harold Owen's account of his experience and says:

Such first-hand accounts as this and many others recorded with such detail and sincerity cannot be ignored, whatever interpretation we put on them. We may note here that the appearance was made some time after the death of Wilfred, which had occurred before the Armistice. One explanation might be that the impression of Wilfred's death had been communicated by telepathy to Harold by his family's shock and gloom on hearing the news on Armistice Day and that this impression had developed in the subconscious mind to produce at last the hallucination at the point when he went into his cabin to write letters home. Those who feel convinced of the survival of human personality after death might be inclined to take a different view.

19

The Ghost of Grandfather Bull

THE EARL OF BALFOUR
AND J. G. PIDDINGTON

The children were nervous and restless in a wretched candle-lit cottage in Wiltshire one evening in February 1932. Three of them had been moved downstairs a fortnight previously from the room in which their grandmother, Mrs Jane Bull, was bedridden. Their mother, Mrs Edwards, was worried because the eldest child, Mary, aged thirteen, had influenza; some of the rooms were not fit to live in, and nine people, including five children, were crowded together in squalor. Now the children, unable to sleep, were complaining that there was someone outside the door.

Mrs Edwards went to the door but no one was there. Her children could not be persuaded to settle down, however, and the conditions that had made them nervous continued.

A little later the reason for the children's nervousness became apparent.

The apparition of their grandfather, Samuel Bull, went up the stairs and through a door which was shut into the room in which he had died and in which his widow had been living until it was condemned as unsafe. This room was now empty.

The children screamed in terror. No wonder. Here was their grandfather, seemingly solid, and dressed as he usually was in the evenings after he had finished his work as a chimney-sweep; but he had died eight months previously of sooty cancer after a four years' illness in which he had been nursed by his wife.

Mrs Edwards and Mary saw the apparition together, and

when he was told, James Bull, the dead man's twenty-one-year-old grandson, confirmed that he, too, could see the figure.

The apparition went to the bedside of his widow and placed his hand, firm but cold, upon her forehead.

When Mrs Bull heard that other members of the family had seen the apparition she confessed that this was not the first time she had seen the figure.

It was not until the apparition disappeared that Mrs Edwards who had been more frightened than the children by the appearance of her dead father, began to feel more composed.

After this the apparition of the dead man appeared frequently to his family at all times of the day and night. The apparition did not glide but walked, made no sound, spoke only once when he called his widow 'Jane', was clearly recognized (even the smallest girl, aged about five, knew this was 'Grandpa Bull'). and once, according to Mrs Edwards, must have been visible for half an hour continuously.

Mrs Edwards was fascinated by the knuckles, which seemed to protrude through the skin – this was the only grisly touch. Later, when questioned, she found it difficult to say anything about colour, possibly because of the dim light in the little house which was lit only by candles at night. She was able to see, however, that the muffler he was wearing was different in colour from the rest of his clothes.

The family always knew that what they called 'the presence' was there for half an hour or more before anybody saw the figure. They were conscious of a peculiar restlessness or stirring of expectancy. Mrs Edwards, describing this feeling, said she felt 'as though I am expecting my brother from America, or something like that.'

Sometimes the apparition appeared when Mrs Edwards's husband was at work or the children at school, but those present could always see him and equally well. At night, although they felt his presence, they could not see him without artificial light, at least at first. All the family noticed the sadness of the apparition's appearance and this they ascribed to the squalid conditions in which they were living, but later, when there was a chance that they might move to a council house, he seemed both happier and lighter in appearance, so much so that Mrs Edwards thought she could detect luminosity in the figure at night.

Although the children had screamed when the apparition first appeared, later appearances were received in a state of quiet awe, but they took a great deal out of the family, particularly the dead man's widow.

The haunting came to the notice of Admiral Hyde Parker, a local resident, who on 3 April related it to the Earl of Selborne. Lord Selborne passed on the information to The Society for Psychical Research.

As a result, the local Vicar, the Rev. George H. Hackett, was asked to compile a report based on a questionnaire to be put to the family.

He replied saying that the family gave 'consistent, satisfactory and in most cases quite clear and definite answers' to his questions, but in one or two instances found it difficult to put the experiences into words.

In an extra note the Vicar added that on one occasion at least the appearance lasted for several hours.

By the time the questionnaire was completed arrangements were well advanced for the family to move into a council house, so the Vicar advised that if the SPR wanted to make an investigations on the spot there was no time to be lost. He pointed out that the apparition might cease to appear particularly as the owner intended to put the house into better condition.

On 14 April we arrived to make inquiries on the spot. Before we went to the haunted house we had a conference with Admiral Hyde Parker and the Vicar at the Admiral's home.

We suggested that the whole story might have been concocted by the family to draw attention to the wretched conditions in which they were living and to increase their chance of getting a better house.

The Vicar replied that he believed in the good faith of the witnesses. He also pointed out that any such plot might well have had the opposite effect to that desired, but admitted that the family might, of course, have miscalculated the outcome of a manoeuvre of this kind.

Admiral Hyde Parker took the view that the family were telling the truth.

Other questions revealed that no one outside the family had seen the apparition and that no member of the family was interested in Spiritualism nor had had an experience similar to this haunting.

We then went to the cottage with the Admiral and the Vicar.

It looked even more depressing that usual. The only furniture was the bed in an upstairs room on which Mrs Bull was lying and a single chair, the rest having been taken to the council house into which the family was moving that day. The dilapidated state of the cottage, which had led the local council to condemn some of the rooms as unfit for habitation, was apparent to us.

Mrs Edwards had her youngest child with her when we called and brought her upstairs with her to the sick room.

The whole story was told again in an interview which lasted forty minutes while the little party stood around the old woman's bed. She had last seen the apparition five days previously.

Most of the questions were addressed to Mrs Edwards. This was because of the state of her mother's health, but Mrs Bull did answer one or two questions.

Mrs Edwards impressed us as being a good witness. She answered the questions put to her simply, naturally, readily and briefly.

We were not able to interview Mr Edwards who, with the

rest of the family, had seen the apparition. We left this task to the Vicar.

On 31 May Mr Hackett wrote to say that he had seen the husband that day and that 'Every question was answered as naturally as before and with as much conviction and appearance of truthfulness.'

Both Mr and Mrs Edwards were willing to sign the statement that was drawn up as the result of the interviews.

The haunting had not been continued in the new house.

This account was first published in the *Journal* of the SPR in October 1932. I included it in the collection of cases in *The Unexplained* but have slightly altered the form of presentation for the present volume. Lord Balfour (the second earl) and Mr Piddington were noted figures in the SPR.

I will not analyse this case in as much detail as I did in the earlier book but it is worth noting that the haunting took place in a house in a poor condition into which too many people were crowded. Since *The Unexplained* was published I have investigated two or three other cases in which strange happenings were reported in houses in which people lived in squalor. Possibly such conditions, particularly during the dark nights of winter, help towards the creation and spreading of a feeling of dread. I am not suggesting that what is generally referred to as the 'Bull Case' can be explained away on this account. A great many families live in squalor without being troubled by the persistent appearance of an apparition, but it is worth while, in my opinion, indicating that there is evidence of a spread of what may be called psychical infection under these conditions, although I will not go so far as to liken this to a disease.

I had not noticed until I reread this case that the appearance of the apparition lasted on one occasion at least for several hours. It is well worth noting that the family ascribed the sadness of the apparition's appearance to the poor conditions under which they were living. If they were correct in this conclusion it puts the haunting into the rather rare class of one in which there is evidence of some purpose.

20

Did Harry Price Return?

JOHN BJÖRKHEM

An unusually thin man of middle height who came to the hospital at Lund in southern Sweden on 8 October 1948 was most insistent in his demands that he should be admitted. His name was Östen Erson [a pseudonym]. The hospital authorities did not want to admit him, pointing out the shortage of beds there, and said that he should have sought admission in the neighbouring town of Malmö, where he lived. However, Erson persisted in his request and it was eventually decided on compassionate grounds to admit him.

Erson sought treatment for his emaciated condition; he weighed only 105 pounds. He was thirty-one years old, a textile worker by trade, but for the past six months had worked as a nightwatchman. He had developed irregular living habits, suffered from insomnia and was short of money.

I had been working only one week in the hospital when Erson came to me for examination. He did not know my name. In describing his condition he was mentally alert and clear-headed. There was a fifty per cent chance that some other doctor might have carried out the preliminary examination.

On the day following his admission the patient asked if he could have a personal interview with me. I referred him to the physician in charge of the department, who was my superior and who was responsible for his treatment. However, Erson insisted that he wanted to talk only to me because it was about matters which he did not want to discuss with 'an outsider'.

Here is Erson's story.

Some time at the end of March or the beginning of April he woke in the night and saw a strange gentleman standing a little bowed over the bed. This seemed to him to be completely natural and he was not afraid. The stranger talked to him in a very friendly and personal way but he could not understand what he said because it was in a foreign language, possibly English.

However, Erson understood that the stranger's name was Price and that he was a doctor or engineer or of some similar occupation. 'Price' suddenly disappeared in a way which he could not understand.

After this 'Price' appeared from time to time in the night and even in the morning when it was quite light. He seemed to be as solid as any other person to whom the patient might have been talking. Objects behind him were obscured, he breathed naturally, and his lips and eyelids moved in a completely natural way. His hands were warm. Not only did Erson see him but his wife shared the experience and certainly at least one of the children, a daughter.

The stranger who came in the night did everything he could to make Erson understand him and he [Erson] began to learn a little English so, gradually, he began to grasp, he thought, most of what 'Price' said to him.

'Price' explained that he had just died and when alive had studied ghosts and similar subjects. Erson found increasingly that he could understand 'Price' and in a peculiar way started to talk to him, although he had studied English so little. Conversation took place in a way which the patient could not explain, so it seemed quite natural when 'Price' appeared.

Erson was by nature unusually analytical and liked to carry out experiments. Many times he tried to take a photograph by flashlight when the figure appeared.

On such occasions 'Price' disappeared. When the plates

were developed there were only a few shadows and no clear outlines.

'Price' seemed to be more amused than angry by these attempts to photograph him.

As the relationship developed 'Price' began to give Erson advice on how he should handle certain situations, such as when his daughter was ill. It was 'Price' who insisted that he should go to the hospital at Lund because there he would receive help for his emaciated state.

If he understood 'Price' aright, an infection in the upper part of his backbone could be the cause of his thinness.

On Erson's first night in hospital 'Price' appeared to him and told him that he had come to the right place and that he should relate his experiences to the doctor who had examined him and not to anyone else.

According to 'Price', what had happened and what was going to happen 'would give science something to think about'.

After this Erson slept very well, as he did all the time he was in hospital.

No other patient in Erson's ward reported having seen a strange person there.

The patient denied all knowledge of Harry Price and asked me if I knew of some Englishman of that name who had been occupied with studies of occult phenomena, but I did not give him any information.

Erson had learned from other patients that I worked in the hospital, but when he wanted an interview he would only meet the doctor whom 'Price' had pointed out. Only after that did he understand that I was identical with the doctor who had first examined him.

I wrote down what the patient had told me and details of some other experiences of an hallucinatory character and put the paper in an envelope with his case history.

Two days after this talk with the patient I received a letter

from a professor in Stockholm, J.T., whom I had met quite by
chance six months earlier. We had first met in 1944 and I
found out then, to my surprise, that he knew Harry Price. We
discussed one of his books but in the two or three meetings
since then we never mentioned his name.

The professor said that he had read in the English magazine
Nature that Price had died on 29 March 1948 and went on to
say jokingly that as Price had hunted ghosts all his life he now
had a chance to become one himself if he wanted to.

Erson underwent all possible tests in the clinic, and was sent
to many special departments for examination, but no organic
cause was found for his condition. At the end he was sent, as is
usual in such cases, to a psychiatric clinic, but the details of the
patient's experiences with 'Price' were not included with the
case history, as they had been told to me in confidence and
might in some way have adversely affected him in the future.
Another factor which had decided me not to include these experiences with the case history notes was that they concerned
the possible existence of parapsychological phenomena: these
might have been received with doubt.

The patient was examined by an outstanding psychiatrist
who, naturally, could not discuss with him his unusual experience (with 'Price'). A diagnosis of schizophrenia was reached
on the grounds of the patient's hallucinations. The psychiatrist
recommended that insulin treatment should be given in a
mental hospital. Erson left the hospital on 13 October.

I finished my hospital work on 30 November. One day in the
middle of December I received a telephone call from the chief
physician in the mental hospital. He said he had telephoned
me many times before but, because I was working elsewhere, I
could be reached only in the late evening. He told me that
Erson had come to the hospital a few days earlier for special
treatment: the diagnosis was schizophrenia made in the psychiatric clinic. The chief physician wanted to compliment me

on what he considered to be 'the excellent case history' I had written. According to him, Erson's illness could be some kind of encephalitis and this could be the cause of his emaciation. As the chief physician did not seem to have heard about Erson's hallucinations I made a copy of my notes on this aspect of the case and sent them to him. After that I heard nothing.

Incidentally, this particular doctor had for many years been a strong opponent of studies in parapsychology.

No evidence was found of schizophrenia. What attitude the chief physician of the mental hospital took after he heard of the patient's hallucinations is not known.

As I did not wish to disturb in any way the spontaneous development of the case I did not make contact again with Erson before January 1951.

He said that 'Price' told him before he went to the hospital at Lund that no factual diagnosis could be made in the medical clinic there. However, this was necessary as it was the only way in which he could be sent to the mental hospital and that was why he was willing to go there.

Erson did have the chance of getting the necessary treatment for his emaciation at the mental hospital, where the chief physician took a special interest in him, later helping him to get housing accommodation.

When Erson was in hospital his weight went up but after that he became thin again.

Even after his stay in Lund 'Price' had sometimes appeared to him.

The more one came to know Erson the more clearly one noticed that his intelligence was noticeably above average, that he had reached an unusually subjective standard of judgement and that, as the years went by, his general view of life had deepened and widened.

His experiences did not change his day-to-day way of thinking and feeling as they would have done if they had been schizophrenic or paranoid hallucinations. However, one could certainly establish that Erson a few years earlier had had some experiences of an hallucinatory nature and that this had given him a certain interest in parapsychological phenomena.

I believe there was a possible physical cause for Erson's emaciation.

If people fast a great deal they get hallucinations of the same type as Erson's. It is worth mentioning that pilots of aircraft get similar hallucinations through lack of oxygen.

In March 1949 I met a person who was well acquainted with the state of psychical studies in England. I said that I heard that Harry Price was dead, but he told me that this was not so and that for various reasons he could remember with certainty that Harry Price was alive. A few months later another person who knew about psychical affairs in England assured me that Harry Price was still alive. I made direct contact with the SPR which informed me that Harry Price had died on 29 March 1948.

As far as I can ascertain, there has been no information in Swedish newspapers about Harry Price's death, at least in such papers to which Erson could have had access.

Was it therefore coincidence which had thrown these separate occurrences together? Why should a professor in Stockholm tell me that Harry Price was dead at the same time as a patient who did not have any idea of Price's existence was informing me that he had received nocturnal visits from 'him' at the actual time of his death? The patient was examined in our most modern clinic but the experts could not agree about his illness. A chief physician telephoned me to say that the previous experts had made a wrong diagnosis although it was quite unlikely that a doctor of his standing should waste his time, from his viewpoint, on such a trivial matter. Were all these happenings a coincidence or does there exist an organizing will behind them? If one can believe that there exists such an organizing will why should Harry Price, at the time of his death, come to a textile worker in Malmö who could not understand what he said and what reaction could he have had from him?

Did 'Price' want, as he said to Erson, to give science something to think about?

Now we come to a whole row of questions: the more one asks the more impossible it is to answer them. One can take the view that nothing like this has happened; or one has to believe that, in the main, various events have happened in the way they have been related here. When viewed separately these events do not have any significance, and it is not until they are connected with one another that they assume a coherence against which criticism becomes uncertain and one gropes after a parapsychological hypothesis.

As people we are still so shortsighted and our knowledge is fragmentary. Sometimes, too, there is little humility.

The above extract comes from *Det Ockulta Problemet* by Dr John Björkhem (J. A. Lindblads Forlag, Uppsala 1951). It has been translated from the Swedish. The book has been published in Germany but not in England.

The case first came to my attention in a review of Dr Björkhem's book by Professor C. D. Broad, who knew the author, in the *Journal* of the SPR for January-February 1953. Professor Broad gave a summary of the case and ended by saying: 'Enough of it has been given to indicate its extreme queerness; and, like Dr Björkhem himself, I do not know what to make of it. It just confirms the platitude that the world is a very odd place and that there are very odd people and events in it.'

First, about the author. Dr Broad said that Dr Björkhem was a man of great learning and wide experience. He had studied and taken degrees in theology, philosophy and medicine. At the time when the review appeared (1953) he was practising as a psychotherapist in Stockholm. He died in 1963.

Now about Harry Price. He died suddenly of a heart attack when smoking a pipe after lunch at his home near London on 29 March 1948. He was sixty-seven. In psychical research circles he was a controversial figure but his books, particularly those about Borley Rectory, are still widely read. I do not think it is unfair to say that his reputation does not stand as high today as it did when he died.

What has puzzled me, and others, about the extraordinary story told in Dr Björkhem's book is that no clues have been provided to enable later researchers to make their own inquiries about the case. The patient is referred to as Ö.E. (I have provided the pseudonym Erson). We are told that Erson's wife and at least one of the children saw the apparition but we are not told if the author interviewed them, as any competent British psychical researcher would have done, to get their account of these strange happenings. I have tried hard, with the help of Mr Inge Sandström, a retired schoolteacher, of Malmö, and Mr Hans Sjöbäck, research assistant at the laboratory of psychology at Lund University, to make progress with the case, but without success. Dr Björkhem told one inquirer, I gather, that Erson is dead.

Dr Björkhem was always very reticent about the case, but this is understandable, to a certain extent, because a doctor-patient relationship was involved. I wrote to Dr Björkhem's widow, Mrs Dagny Björkhem, to see if she could throw any light on the case. She replied that she did not know the address of Ö.E.'s family but, even if she knew, she did not think it would be fair of her to tell me, as her husband had promised the man that he and his family would never be disturbed again with questions about this.

Mrs Björkhem ended her letter by saying: 'My husband treated his patients in a very special way, and it was of great importance to him that they knew they could always trust him and his given word absolutely. So even if the chapter on the Harry Price case is fascinating, I am afraid you can't come further with it.'

Let us now consider whether Erson could have heard any-thing about Harry Price before 1948. Opportunities to do so were undoubtedly available. Mr Sandström, a member of the SPR, pointed out to me that when Erson was twenty years old (in 1937) there was in Sweden a widely circulated coloured weekly *Levande Livet* (Living Life) which contained a series of articles by Harry Price, described as 'England's and perhaps the world's foremost expert in ghostly disturbances'. The name of the series was 'A ghost hunter's adventures'. Mr Sandström added: 'This weekly was to be found in almost all cafés, tea-rooms and canteens at that time and it would be strange if Ö.E., who was interested in occult things, had not seen or read this paper.' Harry Price was also mentioned in the daily press as the 'great ghost hunter'.

Also, we must remember that Harry Price went on lecture tours of Scandinavia in 1925 and 1927.

However, if Erson had opportunities to read about Harry Price as a 'ghost hunter', had he heard about his death? Dr Björkhem obviously did not until later in the year and even then there were so many conflicting reports about it that he had to write to the SPR in London for confirmation.

Mr Sandström said, in a letter dated 17 June 1965: 'When I first read this case I was quite sure that I had seen a short announcement in a Swedish paper about Harry Price's death. Now I have gone through many papers of April 1948 but have not found the few lines about the famous ghost hunter's death. Perhaps it was mentioned later, perhaps my memory has failed me.'

In an article in the September 1963 issue of the *Journal* of the SPR Dr John Beloff, lecturer in psychology at Edinburgh

abl
Was
ps

JAN 20 75
FEB 17 75

_____
Keep this card in the book pocket
Book is due on the latest date stamped
Book is due on the latest date stamped
Keep this card in the book pocket
_____

133.1
M15
MacKenzie, Andrew.
A gallery of ghosts.
c.1

CHICAGO HEIGHTS FREE PUBLIC LIBRARY

15TH ST. & CHICAGO ROAD

CHICAGO HEIGHTS, ILL.

60411

PHONE SKyline 4-0323